S0-AWN-181

ENDORSEMENT

Evelyn Watkins has written a practical roadmap to your new beginning. *Your Next Chapter* offers a fresh perspective for all who face life's ups and downs while providing strategies to achieve happiness in spite of what life throws your way.

EDWARD M. HALLOWELL, M.D.
New York Times bestselling author of *Driven to Distraction*

YOUR

NEXT ——

CHAPTER

YOUR

N E X T —

CHAPTER

[*Re-Writing Your Life Success Story*]

EVELYN D. WATKINS

— Life and Business Recovery Coach —

© Copyright 2013–Evelyn D. Watkins

All rights reserved. This book is protected by the copyright laws of the United States of America. This book may not be copied or reprinted for commercial gain or profit. The use of short quotations or occasional page copying for personal or group study is permitted and encouraged. Permission will be granted upon request.

Sound Wisdom

P.O. Box 310

Shippensburg, PA 17257-0310

For more information on foreign distribution, call 717-530-2122.

Reach us on the Internet: www.soundwisdom.com.

ISBN 13 TP: 978-1-937879-32-7

ISBN 13 Ebook: 978-1-937879-33-4

For Worldwide Distribution, Printed in the U.S.A.

2 3 4 5 6 7 8 / 16 15 14

CONTENTS

DEDICATION

THIS BOOK IS DEDICATED TO EVERY PERSON WHO HAS HIT A dead end, brick wall, or lost love. I hope you find the courage to rescue yourself, give way to a new dream, and compose your new life success story.

INTRODUCTION

THE GOAL OF THIS BOOK IS TO PROVIDE YOU WITH PRACTI-cal methods to rescue yourself, begin writing your new story, and celebrate your subsequent success. My goal is for this resource to be an interactive support tool which by book's end will have produced a working plan for your new success story.

> *The best way to predict the future
> is to invent it.* —ALAN KAY

Chapter 1

WHAT YOU WILL GET FROM THIS BOOK

Never mistake motion for action.

—ERNEST HEMINGWAY

WE COME OF AGE WITH A LIFE PLAN FOR SUCCESS. THE plan may include marriage, retirement from the company your dad worked and retired from, or a successful business—and the list goes on. But what inevitably happens is life. Life happens and things change. You get the dreaded cancer diagnosis, maybe the marriage falls apart, you never had the baby you always dreamed you would, or like millions of Americans you find yourself unemployed or underemployed. The bottom line—this is not the "happily ever after" you imagined. It is not the story of success you planned.

I considered calling this book *Plan B*. Everyone understands that concept and has had to rely on their own Plan B. But what I have concluded is that there are many of us who have surpassed Plan B, C, D, E, F, and G. There aren't enough letters in the alphabet to represent the number of plans we go through when trying to get back on track. If we are to thrive, we must find the track and get on it.

The beauty of our country's recent recession is that it joined most people in a way that they were not before. Everyone understood the importance of having a plan. A financial plan, a family plan, a health plan, and an exit plan. It also unveiled a host of dirty secrets.

We've amassed houses we cannot afford and cars we should have never been driving. We carry purses that cost as much as our car payment, and our solid job is not so solid after all. We discovered our marriages under pressure didn't hold up so well, and the complications of life only exacerbate our fragile futures. We're left vulnerable, exposed with two choices—wait until total destruction or begin writing a new success story.

Inaction is death. Unconscious living without a strategy to succeed—unacceptable. Waiting for a rescue plan is futile; your rescue plan is inside you.

Together we will uncover your rescue plan—your stimulus plan the government cannot provide. It requires your passion, your plan, your progress, and your pursuit. In the end, your new chapter may read better than the empty story you had planned before.

> *Parents have proven to be a convenient third party to blame for all the things you don't want to blame on yourself.*

Chapter 2

OWNING YOUR CHOICES

There are two primary choices in life: to accept conditions as they exist, or accept the responsibility for changing them. —DENIS WAITLEY

WHEN YOU LOOK AT A MAP AT THE MALL, BEFORE YOU can get to the store of your desire you have to find the "you are here" marker. So as we begin this process of writing a new chapter for our lives and defining our new destination, we have to first begin with the "you are here" marker. To be effective in making it to the next destination, we have to identify where we are, If we are to progress again and again, it helps to understand how you got there. Starting at the marker in the mall is no good if you don't know how to get out of the mall or find your way back to the marker. One part alone will only offer a portion of success. We must endeavor to know all three—where we are, how we arrived here, and the map to our next destination.

One of the most difficult realizations I've made in my life is the truth of my choices. Be it a poor relationship or dead-end job, I seemed to find myself feeling like a victim, wondering, *How did I get here? Why is this happening to me? Where did I go wrong?*

I had that very conversation with myself. With great anguish, I did my best to analyze my life—my choices, my part. *I'm smart,* I thought. *Smart enough to have been prepared for the worst; smart enough to have successfully avoided the worst.* Yet I stood like many others in the same empty place, feeling bad for myself and wanting desperately to get out. The problem was I really didn't know how.

If you're a real estate agent who loves the hustle and satisfaction of closing the deal, discovering that the market is dried up can be disheartening. If you're a school teacher who has been subjected to district cuts, you may be wondering where to place that passion for training and educating others. Or maybe you're a spouse who never expected to be alone, and now during the worst economic period of our time you've been served with divorce papers.

Whether job loss, relationship loss, or the loss of a loved one, the stages of disappointment and grief are pretty much the same. Shock and denial happen during the first stage of grief—the shock of discovering the behaviors of an unfaithful spouse, or the disbelief at the loss of a loved one or having the rug pulled out from under you when losing a job.

After weeks of working overtime through the Thanksgiving and Christmas holiday I was bracing myself for a bonus as the vice president of human resources and the executive vice president asked for a moment of my time. I sat poised, prepared to act surprised as they adorned me with my well-deserved bonus or raise. After all, since the company's recent acquisition, I alone worked late each evening, preparing documents and methodologies for the merging of the two firms.

The announcement of the merger had just happened days earlier, and now the real transition was in sight. My boss began, "You really are such a wonderful asset to our team."

I thought, *Yeah, yeah, blah, blah, blah...let's just get to the money, okay?*

My anxiousness turned to anxiety when I heard him say, "I'm really sorry to tell you that we have to let you go."

I sat stunned but quickly put a grin on my face—I guess to make them more comfortable with giving me the axe. The irony of it all is quite hilarious today. The same irony has been true many other times. I found myself expecting reward only to discover I would be denied my sense of stability or peace. The timing of that particular layoff was painful, because at the time my husband had not worked for about eight months. My immediate panic was fortunately subdued when my husband received a job offer just days later. Nevertheless, the shock of the moment and subsequent denial can become paralyzing.

There are some things we cannot change. If a loved one dies, clearly you can't change that outcome. You can perhaps recover from the sense of guilt you feel if there are words you failed to say or some unfinished work, but changing the outcome is not an option. Life-altering shifts, however—such as the breakup of a marriage or joblessness—we can redo. We can recover, and if we are daring enough we can attempt the same endeavor with a different outcome. But we have to first figure out how we arrived in that place.

The truth is, we have to own our part. We play a part in our broken relationships, marriages, failures, and the endgame of our job loss. We were participants who assisted in the development of our own disappointment, and sometimes our demise.

So let's begin by facing the facts. We own our choices. We own our part. Embracing that truth can be liberating because it forces us to transcend from the place of a helpless victim to an empowered victor. Like a child who has been assaulted, a victim was merely present. Things happened around that person over which he or she had no control. Victims are not participants, they are objects of someone else's actions. When you discover you are not a victim, it is empowering because it demonstrates that your participation is required. Therefore, if you choose to be a victor, you merely have to change your participation strategy.

As I assessed the adversity I sometimes faced in marriage, I really did feel as though I was "punked" in many ways. When your life doesn't unfold as you expect or you come to realize that your spouse isn't *you* at all, but your spouse is in fact flawed, you may feel as though you were tricked or handed the short end of the stick. This kind of thinking negates the fact that you are a chooser. To suggest "the short end of the stick" implies that you made a choice without being informed. I know that I have made informed choices throughout my adult life. Thus, it is not possible to be overtaken by something or someone when you had the knowledge.

Many people contend with feeling like a single parent when they thought they married a partner; feeling like a housekeeper when they discover their partner refuses to do housework; or feeling like a sex object if they discover their partner doesn't have the capacity to be faithful. No matter the scenario, you are not a victim in the relationship. You did, in fact, take part in choosing your spouse as much as that person chose you.

If you actively overlooked the obvious signs, it is no surprise that you can now reassess the early stages of your relationship and see exactly what was there all along and why you chose to ignore it. The same can be said for taking a job that you knew didn't suit your life-style or wasn't something you were passionate about. Yet you took it anyway, and now find yourself miserable and feeling trapped as the years wear on.

So let us begin at the beginning. Take a quick assessment of your part in choosing to be where you are today. Do you know your part already? You may have to ponder for a bit to see your truth, but you must see it. It took me a while to be honest about my part in my own downfalls. At first I wouldn't admit it out loud, but once I recognized my part and owned it, I could forgive myself and say, "You're going to do better next time, girl!"

Journal this process. Seeing the words on paper is a powerful tool to support your progress. Now it's time to begin writing your new chapter!

> *The broken become masters at mending.* —MIKE MURDOCK

C h a p t e r 3

ALL CRACKED UP: SIFTING THROUGH THE BROKEN PLACES

> The world breaks everyone and afterward many are strong in the broken places. But those that will not break, it kills. It kills the very good and the very gentle and the very brave impartially. If you are none of these you can be sure it will kill you too but there will be no special hurry. —ERNEST HEMINGWAY

HEMINGWAY SAID, "THE WORLD BREAKS EVERYONE." I LOVE that quote so much, because life does break you. In brokenness you are vulnerable, teachable, and willing to believe. It is during this time you may find yourself becoming more humble and willing to ask for help. Many perceive this process as a visible weakness. I perceive it as visibly human.

If you've ever had a favorite cup that had a crack in it, you probably discovered that you can still successfully drink from it. The crack may taint what you are drinking; perhaps you have residue of the ceramic cup in your beverage, but for the most part you can probably get away with the crack. You are aware of its existence, but you're still able to do life as usual. That's what many of us have done—live a life with a crack, hoping it doesn't fall apart. But eventually the crack will be compromised and the cup will break. We have all experienced breaks to varying degrees, some greater than others. As Hemingway writes so beautifully, "Afterward, many are strong in the broken places." Nothing in life teaches like an experience. Regardless of the root of your crack or the reason you are broken, the experience has taught you much. Now you have the opportunity to be stronger in those areas.

I have a friend who has overcome cancer three times. With each presentation of the new diagnosis, she was more resilient, resolved, and determined to live. She learned coping skills after the first diagnosis. She learned how to take a sucker punch when she thought she was "out of the woods" the second time. And the third time, she really learned how to take control of her life by sacrificing part of her body in exchange for receiving confidence concerning her future. With very difficult choices, she decided to pick up the pieces and demand a different future, a new chapter. She now gives encouragement to others through lectures, writings, and support groups. She learned how to be strong in the broken places.

When I gave birth to my first daughter Gabrielle, I was still wading in the pool of callousness my life had produced. I am the sixth child of nine who found herself in the foster care system at the age of six. My mother remained in a coma for 14 years before dying at the age of 46. Through my multiple foster homes, I learned to rely only on myself. I discovered at a young age that strangers could not be trusted and family could be worse than an adversary. So when Gabrielle was born, it seemed natural to endure motherhood alone. I lived in Atlanta, miles away from my Massachusetts roots and the family and friends I nurtured over the years. I assumed every responsibility, from feeding to housekeeping, bathing, and the like. It was my job.

My husband found his place in all of this and it was, by my own training, to do as little as possible. Others reached out to help me but I declined, thinking I wouldn't want to owe them anything. When my second daughter Noelle was born, she had a few gastrointestinal challenges which required her to sleep sitting up and take medication.

Although Gabrielle was colicky for the first 12 weeks of her life, she had no one else competing with her for my attention. Noelle's challenges hindered my ability to take care of Gabrielle adequately and exaggerated my need for help. I witnessed her arms and legs flailing as she tried to eject the fluid from the back of her throat. I was afraid to lay her down because she often choked from vomiting and could not recover well in a horizontal position. It was scary to watch. That ended the idea of her sleeping flat or sleeping alone. I remember sitting up with her one night, and as she rested on my upright chest, I thought, *I can't do this again.* A few times I thought I would just lose it because I was so tired. Noelle slept on my chest until she was about four months old. My sister April flew in to help me shortly after Noelle was born. She cooked, played endlessly with Gabrielle, and even gave me a pedicure. It was a humbling process for me, but one which demonstrated her compassion and my humanity.

To witness humanity oftentimes means one does so by witnessing humility. In my weakness, I was able to be strengthened by another because I recognized my own limitations and received the support I needed. In doing so, I was able to piece together how I would thrive with the new challenges I faced.

I pieced together how my parenting style would have to change, how I would have to solicit and receive support, how I would have to dismantle the crown of "Every Woman" and realize I was still human, in need of rest and emotional rejuvenation. Furthermore, no one was going to hand out a medal if I did everything myself. My reward needed to come from within, and it would begin by recognizing that what I had done before was not an option. I would need to reward my life and the life of my new daughter with a new cup. The cracked one would no longer hold up. It had been compromised and was now broken. Not destroyed—simply broken. There was still the opportunity to pick up the pieces and begin anew.

This is your chance. Wherever you are—jobless, homeless, separated from your family—you still have a pulse; therefore, you still have purpose. You still have a chance to reassemble your life and redeem your present situation. You have not been destroyed. Maybe humbled, maybe broken, but not destroyed. So your manuscript begins right now. It starts with you beginning the process of picking up the pieces that remain.

> *Nobody can go back and start a new beginning, but anyone can start today and make a new ending.* —MARIA ROBINSON

Chapter 4

FORCED CHANGE: REALIZING THE GROUND HAS SHIFTED

The future has a way of arriving unannounced. —GEORGE WILL

WHEN I BEGAN THE PROCESS OF WRITING A NEW CHAPTER for my life, it wasn't because I was excited about the future. It wasn't because I was independently wealthy and wanted something to do with my spare time. Instead, I was forced to change because my circumstances had changed. I took a part-time job at a health care facility because I developed a chronic condition which required me to see a specialist and purchase expensive medicine. I needed exceptional health insurance and that part-time job afforded me just that. It was forced—not really a choice but more of a mandate.

I began investing my time in technical writing and training because I couldn't find other work. In doing so, I discovered I possessed talents I was unaware of until that time. Again, the market had changed. I was forced to create my own opportunity because there were no available opportunities waiting for me. I began to make smarter decisions concerning my finances, parenting style, and marriage. Again, not because I had an insightful epiphany, but because the ground had shifted and required me to think and act differently.

I recall a story of a woman who was about to lose her house to foreclosure and began baking cakes. She only had one particular cake she was selling, and did so at $40 apiece. A local business heard of her story and partnered with her to utilize their facility to bake the cakes. Within a few weeks, she sold enough to make one of the payments the bank required to stop the process of foreclosure. Within three months, she was able to catch up on her mortgage payments and gave birth to a new business. There are talks of her offering the cake on QVC. I don't know if this woman ever intended to start a cake business, but the business was birthed out of a desperate situation. The ground had shifted for this new entrepreneur and she was forced to do something different. Perhaps something radical. Her radical change helped save her house and demonstrated a talent she possessed all along.

I've met countless people who didn't intend to ruin their credit. People who never expected their spouse to be unfaithful or to leave them. People who always intended to go back to school but put their family needs ahead of their own personal growth and now find themselves unemployable. People who have lost jobs or feel threatened with job loss and never gave thought to a Plan B. People who never thought they'd be the one with cancer. And although life is filled with unexpected setbacks, our new 21st-century solutions seem remarkably different from those of the 20th century. Things have changed dramatically. People look younger; younger people are smarter and far more educated; people are bolder and much more assertive. In short, the competition is overwhelmingly great and the choices seem meager.

So as you take on the daunting task of assessing what changes you need to make, you have to recognize what kind of changes have already been made around you. For example, seeking a job right now in investment banking may not be as easy as it was in the 1990s. The same could be said for real estate, acquisition management, and with the transfer of jobs overseas even the IT field seems vulnerable. So you have to recognize how your progression is impacted by current realities. There are people who hate the relationship they are in but feel trapped due to their inability to financially support themselves and their children. Perhaps, like me, you have found that you are unemployable or are presently underemployed. Landing that *great* new job may not be a reality in this present market, therefore, you may have to create your own opportunity.

Take the time to assess where you are and what kind of changes you need to make. We will figure out the details of how you will actually change in the pages ahead; for now, just write down what kind of changes you are forced to make due to your current realities. Additionally, what changes do you want to make? Both changes are important, they simply happen at different times.

If your house is about to foreclose and you have no savings, asserting that you want to begin a savings plan may not do anything to change your immediate situation. But if you are in a dead-end job and want to begin something new, you can begin taking steps on the new prospect while you are working to fund your new opportunity with clothes, classes, business license or fees, etc.

I have a friend who endured a pretty ugly divorce. She had endured her husband's infidelity longer than she was willing to admit. She had children and felt too financially vulnerable to leave her spouse. She began devising a plan to depart. It was quiet and unknown by anyone around her. When she knew she had a safe place to live, secured a better job, and could take care of herself, she surprised him and took him up on his offer of divorce. The decision was not without the expected heartbreak and divisive calamity, but because she responded to what had changed in her life and planned around it, she and her children were able to overcome this difficult time intact.

Don't be discouraged at the change you are embarking on, even if it is forced. Like the new cake maker, you may discover better relationships, better career opportunities, and a richer life as a result of being forced to do something you would not have done without the push.

Take a few moments to answer the following:

1. What kind of change would you like to make?

2. What is holding you back from making the change you desire?

3. What change are you forced to respond to?

4. What are you doing right now in response to the forced change around you?

5. List three things you can begin to address in response to the forced change in your life.

> *Your life mission is not your decision
> but instead your discovery.*

Chapter 5

DEFINING YOUR NEW LIFE MISSION

People wanted a statement; I decided to be a
statement. —KATHIE LEE GIFFORD, discussing
the media awaiting statements about her
marriage following her husband's infidelity

ONE OF THE MOST REMARKABLE REVELATIONS I'VE MADE concerning my own life is the power of words to shape my self-perception and self-esteem. I spent most of my adolescent years feeling fat, dumb, and destined for unwed pregnancy or alcoholism—mostly because those were messages spoken to me on a regular basis. Later in my teen years, I pretended with my peers that I was fabulous, confident, self-assured, and unmoved by the thoughts of others. I was none of those things, yet in my pretense something strange began to happen. I began to become what I repeated and pretended.

I didn't pay much attention to this transformation until years later. My siblings were scattered throughout the city in various foster homes. Although we didn't share stories growing up, we did have a few things in common—most of us had endured diverse forms of abuse. As I sat around with my siblings reflecting on our childhoods, I pondered how we escaped conforming into the atrocities we experienced. We were determined to be better, defy our surroundings, and be what no one thought we could—successful.

Our journeys were colored both by our thoughts and our words. I asserted mantras for different seasons of my life. There were times when I simply had to believe I would survive; thus my mantra or mission statement was, "I will survive." Once I became a survivor, my mantra changed and so did I.

As I aged and evolved I came to understand the importance of a focused mission or life mission. More than a mantra, a life mission statement evokes your purpose and intent. Much more powerful than a title, it defines your *raison d'etre*, or reason for being.

It's a powerful message for you to see and a connecting message to draw others. Much like the quote at the beginning of this chapter, your objective is to *be a statement*. Your mission statement may evolve as you do with seasons, age, or conditions. Women in particular may find difficulty nailing down a life mission statement. They have difficulty in seeing their purpose outside of their primary roles or titles. The first lesson in developing a meaningful life mission statement is to realize that you are *more than your title*. You are more than someone's supervisor. You are more than someone's father or mother. You are more than someone's wife or husband. You are more than a title. This line of thinking is not meant to diminish the significance and value of your title, but instead to challenge you to acknowledge the depth and breadth of your purpose beyond your title.

I implore you to create your life mission statement. Remember, it should speak to your intent and purpose and not simply what you are capable of right now. For example, you may say, "My life mission statement is to *provide job skills to women in shelters* or *write novels that give readers an escape.*" The statement may not speak to what is transpiring right now in your life; however, it speaks to your intent, your desire, and your possibilities.

After you compose your life mission statement, take this initiative a step further. Print it. I recommend you find some inexpensive business cards at your local office supply store and print the cards with your name, life mission statement, and telephone number.

I remember an author of children's stories—well actually, at the time she began calling herself an author she only had titles of the books she would eventually write. She began carrying business cards with her life mission statement on them: "Writing children's books to inspire young leaders." Everywhere she went, rather than hand out her business card from her employer she'd hand out her life mission statement card. After a while, people began connecting her to others who were able to support her mission—illustrators, editors, agents, and a local talent booker for a television program. The more she'd hand out the card and talk about her dream, the more motivated she was to finally write the stories. By the time she completed the stories, she had a network of supporters and suppliers prepared to produce and market her books.

Some people find having a visual picture helpful—photos from magazines or of other people who are living a similar life to the one you desire. You can put them on a board, frame it, and put it on a refrigerator or bathroom mirror. Remember, your objective is to create a statement so you can become the statement. Whatever it takes to create a focused mission, you should do. Make it plain, easy to understand, easy to believe, and easy for others to see how they can support you.

> *A good plan today is better than*
> *a perfect plan in the future.*

Chapter 6

PREPARING FOR YOUR BIG MOVE

> The will to win is worthless if you do not
> have the will to prepare. —THANE YOST

So you're thinking about taking the big step—quitting your job, ending a relationship, or starting that book. Failing to plan is planning to fail. You have to have a plan. Perhaps the plan is to spend several months saving a nest egg so you won't be so vulnerable. How are you to do that if you're already strapped? With a plan and a strategy.

Hopelessness and helplessness often occur as a result of feeling as though you have no options. At this very moment, perhaps you don't have palpable options, but you *always* have options, you simply choose not to use the ones you have right now! You are not trapped; you simply choose not to utilize the options you possess today. It is quite empowering. The way to overcome feeling hopeless is by increasing your options so you don't feel like a victim but you become one who is committed to a plan and a strategy.

If you are in a dead-end job and feel as though it is the only job you'll ever have, that can be a depressing concept. If instead you concluded that you have a nine-month or two-year plan to transfer, obtain skills to find new employment, or begin a new business, you may discover you have the wherewithal to withstand the drudgery of the job for a short period.

So a plan offers encouragement that things will not always remain the same. That there is fluidity to your life and things are in movement. It's encouraging to know that you won't have to live with your parents forever, or that the emotionally abusive relationship you are in is not the only possibility of love you'll ever know. It, too, is subject to change; you simply must plan for the change.

Preparation breeds peace. When you make certain you fill your empty tank before you park your car in the garage in the evening, it provokes peace the next morning when you start it up, because you don't fear running out of gas or running late by filling up during rush hour. Tourism hot spots take advantage of your desire to possess this peace of mind as they attempt to sell you all-inclusive trips so you need not worry about bringing cash for meals or other incidentals.

How much more must you prepare for the big things in life? Major disability from a catastrophic illness? Divorce? Repossessed car? Foreclosure? Joblessness? As difficult as the life-altering episodes are, you will be able to endure them much easier with a plan.

There is a proverb which says, "The ants are a people not strong, yet they prepare their meat in the summer." Now, I don't believe people are like ants. In fact, Eleanor Roosevelt remarked so beautifully, "A woman [person] is like a teabag—you don't know how strong she is until you put her in hot water." I love that quote and find it exceedingly true, but like the ant, we too must prepare our *meat* in the summer. Just when it looks like a good time to rest, we've got to get preparing. Just when we've convinced ourselves we deserve a spa day, we've got to get preparing. Have you ever noticed how short the summer feels? It seems to fly right by. But the winter, oh dear—sometimes it seems like it lasts for half a year. The ant knows this by instinct. It knows the winter could be long and harsh and prepares for the worst. We must do the same, recognizing that our big move, our big transition could be long and harsh, so we must prepare for the worst. In doing so, we will increase our peace.

So let us imagine your hard time is at hand; presume it will be long and harsh. What are the initial steps you need to take to prepare for your big move? I recommend you use a calendar—a big one. I know during this age of electronic calendars and the like, it may seem a bit rudimentary to utilize an old-fashioned calendar, however, I recommend its use for the sake of its visual usefulness. Take a look at the current month in your calendar and begin to write down small tasks you can take on each week. Putting away a few dollars each Tuesday or making new posts on your social media networks. Your preparation should include a clear strategy with a clear path of progression. Look at the framework below and complete it as best as you can with your own information.

CONDENSED STRATEGY OUTLINE

I.   *Objective (Example: begin dessert delivery business)*

II.   *Investments Required*

      1.   Indicate how much money you need to meet your objective.

- Develop a doable plan to set aside or raise funds to meet your objective.

- Consider selling your unused inventory of jewelry, clothing, and furniture.

- Consider who you can ask to invest into your endeavor.

- Commit to a date to obtain the initial investment (seed money).

- Establish a separate account or trustworthy person to oversee your funds.

III. Research marketing opportunities to bring attention to your new effort.

1. Job boards, social media

2. Local newspapers

3. Public access television opportunities

4. Writing for blogs (or begin your own)

IV. Network

1. Find local groups or individuals who may support your vision.

   - Your local church

   - Church or community support groups

   - Community classes or membership-driven organizations

   - Business conferences and leadership trainings

- Social media

- If divorcing or experiencing a significant relationship change, you should begin to identify new people who will be able to support your new career needs, housing needs, or perhaps emotional encouragement.

V. Sales Plan

1. Identify your market.

2. Identify your demographic.

3. Commit to a price.

4. Develop a plan to sell yourself (job) or your product to your market.

5. Develop goals.

   - Job goals should have a number of applications submitted during a given period or a number of fairs to attend.

   - Business goals should include an expected revenue by an expected date.

VI. Execute

1. Begin to do what you planned.

   - If selling, begin to sell your product.

   - If applying for a loan, job, or grant, begin to do so.

> *A place for everything, and everything in its place.* —ISABELLA MARY BEETON

Chapter 7

ORGANIZING YOUR BIG BOOM EXPERIENCE

If you can organize your kitchen,
you can organize your life.

I ADMIRE WOMEN WHO, WHEN ASKED FOR THEIR ID, CAN immediately pull at their neatly stuffed wallet—credit cards in all of the proper places, cash in the cash section, and change in the change purse. This mini purse is found cozily in a well organized larger purse which, once opened, can easily display its contents with one quick glance. When looking for keys in my purse, forget it—it'll take several minutes. My wallet *always* has cash in the change purse and my cards never find their way back into their slot immediately after use. It's just my DNA. I am not a naturally organized person. I have a once-a-week purse clean-out session and I am always surprised at the things that have found their way into my leather-bound black hole.

Organization reveals much. It shows us what we have, it provides order to get what we need, and it removes lots of stress along the way.

I love the quote at the beginning of this chapter because it is a wonderful metaphor for the simplicity of organization. Just as I have the once-a-week purse cleaning session, I do the same for my kitchen pantry, refrigerator, and cabinets. Most people who do a great job at maintaining their organization efforts wouldn't have to have this ongoing project. But for folks like me it is a necessity, because neither I nor anyone else in my family seems to have a knack for keeping things orderly enough to neglect this weekly ritual.

Once I complete it, I usually discover that I have two or more of the same item which I purchased because I wasn't aware I already had it. I'm sure you've experienced this too. It is so frustrating to find out that you wasted resources buying things you already possess. Even so, when I prepare to go to the grocery store I am confident about what I have. I'm not vacillating and unsure; I am certain about what I lack and thus what I need to buy.

I've done the same with my closet. Just a few months ago when I organized my closet, I was overwhelmed by the amount of clothes and shoes I have. I hung all of my suits on one side, dresses in another section, pants and skirts and tops in yet another section. Now, I've organized my closet before, but not in this manner. It was an illuminating process. It truly demonstrated my affinity for certain fabrics and colors, and moreover it was a visual exercise in assessing my assets. I truly could see that I had more clothes than I needed. I began mixing and matching outfits in the following weeks and people who I'd seen all the time marveled at my new ensembles. I took great pleasure in letting them know that they were items I had all along.

This process and principle is true in every area of our lives. As you are preparing for big changes, you must get order in your life. It is the only way you can assess what you have and what you need. I have a pretty large closet; in fact, it is the size of a small room. Looking it over can be daunting when considering taking on the task of organizing; however, once started the process flows fairly quickly. Just like the quote at the beginning of the chapter, if you can organize a kitchen, you really can organize your life. You have to get past the observation of the disorder. Past the paper, bank statements, or over-booked calendar. You have to commit to it, and as Nike says, "Just do it."

Begin this process like any other, with a decision. Once you decide to organize, give yourself a series of steps to get the job done.

Remember, achieving milestones will fuel you with the momentum to complete your project. So what do you need to organize right now to get to the next place in your progress? Begin by breaking the project up into smaller pieces that are relatively easy to complete.

I remember telling my daughter Noelle to clean her playroom. It was a mess. Books all over the place, stuffed animals everywhere, Barbie dolls tossed, and paper airplanes crashed throughout. She looked around the room and began to cry. "I'm never going to finish; it's gonna take forever!" she wailed.

That's how we act sometimes when faced with having to clean up our mess. We feel like we're never going to finish, like it's going to take forever. And what do we do? Pretty much what Noelle attempted to do—stop in our tracks, cry, and complete nothing.

After a useless back and forth, I challenged her to complete one task. "Pick up all of the books and put them on the bookcase. Call Mommy when you're all done."

Noelle seemed much happier with this new assignment. "Okay," she replied happily.

Off she went, and she returned quite quickly with the first task done. "Now pick up all of the Barbie dolls and put them in the bin."

Again, "Okay," she replied, and completed the task quite quickly. This went on and on until the playroom was complete. The smaller tasks didn't overwhelm her and she was surprised at her own progress. I use this method with my girls for just about everything because it works and it yields a sense of accomplishment once completed.

You may have to pull out that calendar we previously discussed and begin to schedule dates and milestones to achieve. The key to success is being realistic about what you are capable of and the amount of time it will take for you to fulfill your goal.

If you haven't filed your taxes in the past four years, it may not be realistic that you will be able to gather up all the necessary papers in just a month. If you've been writing poetry on notepads for years, it may take you a while to locate all of those notepads. You may have to re-write your resume or business plan altogether rather than trying to locate which resume you used four years ago.

Your life shouldn't feel like a Big Boom Experience, riddled with disorder awaiting alignment. Take the baby steps to get organized right now. You'll breathe a sigh of relief as the order you create will demonstrate you're probably not lacking nearly as much as you thought. And you may not have to do nearly as much as you feared you would.

> *A big part of financial freedom is having your heart and mind free from worry about the what-ifs of life.* —SUZE ORMAN

Chapter 8

THE SHE MONEY FUND

Money makes the world go around.
—lyrics from musical play *Cabaret*

I'T'S EASY TO GET CAUGHT UP IN THE GOOD TIMES—THE laughter, the good food, the friends. Wine gives sparkle to life; for those who drink wine or champagne, it's celebratory—it's good cheer. But it *is* money that makes the world go around. So at the end of the day, your hospitality doesn't pay the bills, fellowship isn't going to give you health insurance, and good times can turn to difficult times on a dime and then what do you have left?

The economic troubles our nation has recently faced demonstrated that façades cannot pay the bills. I, like many others, have discovered that when the veil was removed and my vulnerability exposed, the cost of continuing life as usual would bankrupt me.

If this economic catastrophe has taught us anything at all, it has demonstrated that the cruise-control mentality is insufficient to secure our tomorrow. Immediate action to assure our economic future is not merely a good idea but a mandate.

Let's look at personal finance from a woman's point of view, for a moment. Pre-boomers believed that a woman's ticket to success was to find a wonderful man to marry. Boomers also believed that a woman could find romantic love and economic security in a spouse, but they heralded the belief that she was a deliberate force in defining her financial strength and professional affluence. Generation X fully embraced the "every woman" idea. As such, these women have methodically planned their lives, assuming massive educational debt, securing homes, purchasing automobiles, joining clubs, and positioning children in great private schools—all while having massages, manicures, and highlights. The truth of our economy has revealed the truth of our own bogus financial security.

I recall hearing a speaker many years ago who introduced me to the term "she money." He was quite funny and explained that "she money" was a little stash of cash that men kept that "she" didn't know about. It was a lighthearted commentary which was made in his wife's presence, and both the men and women in the audience laughed aloud. The fifty dollars this man had hidden deep in a secret place in his wallet represented freedom and power. *Freedom* because he could do what he wished with the money. *Power* because he had the very material that makes the world go around—money.

I have borrowed his term and added a third word—*fund*—because I, like many people, realized that I was in need of both power and freedom. Many people seem to have no difficulty with believing the hype around them. Like, *your spouse is always going to assure things are financially okay.* Or, *your employer would never let you go.*

Or, *you don't need a backup plan for that family business.* Our failure to respect the importance of our money, credit, and financial value has left us much more vulnerable and with fewer choices. It further paralyzes us when we desperately need to make a big move because we lack the resources to do it.

In order to change your power and change your circumstances, you have to start somewhere. Make a decision to open a savings account. Some banks allow you to round up your debit card transactions and the change goes into a savings account—that's another great way to save. If you don't have enough money to open an account, just begin at home with a jar, like many of our grandparents did. The jar can contain coins or dollars; just begin with whatever you have. First $25, then $50, then it grows to $500. I'm telling you, there is nothing more powerful than knowing that you have money, even just a little, to do as *you* wish. It's a little like that child who has a piece of candy that someone gave him and he's hiding it in his pocket. He has a small smirk on his face because no one knows about it. It's just his and he'll save it for just the right time and it will be oh so sweet! That's what having money is like; you may start out small, but simply knowing it's there is just enough to make you smile inside, and at just the right time when you pull it out—oh so sweet!

Be honest with yourself. If you cannot be trusted to save your own money, then give it to a trustworthy friend. Put it in an account where you don't have ATM access. I had an aunt who told me when I was quite young to give her a little money each week—$10, $25—and she would hold it for me. I did just that. Sometimes I'd mail it, sometimes I'd hand it to her. When I made a big move to Atlanta from Massachusetts at the age of 23, I asked her for the money I'd given her. She replied, "What money?"

I told her, "The money I've been giving you every week for the past year or so." She claimed she didn't know what I was talking about. I was annoyed but didn't let it bother me.

Once in Atlanta, I depleted my retirement from my previous state employment and began taking cash advancements on my credit cards to live. Shortly thereafter, I landed a job and then an apartment. I went home to visit over the holidays and my aunt went to her attic to give me towels and other household necessities for my apartment.

She then handed me a check for the total amount of the cash I had given her, plus interest. She smiled at me and said, "I told you I wasn't going to give it back to you," but now of course she knew I needed it and the timing couldn't have been more perfect. Had I received the money earlier I certainly would have squandered it, but now I couldn't have been more grateful for her diligent stewardship over my savings.

Every person needs a "she money fund"—money you have set aside and are not spending. Get started today; your financial peace is waiting for you.

> *An investment in knowledge*
> *pays the best interest.*
> —BENJAMIN FRANKLIN

Chapter 9

INVESTING IN YOUR LIFE

The most important investment you can
make is in yourself. —WARREN BUFFET

I KNEW A WOMAN WHO STRUGGLED WITH HER WEIGHT ALL OF her adult life. She really wanted to lose the weight but needed a support system to get it done. I recall talking to her about places like Quick Weight Loss Centers and Nutri-System because I knew of other women who had terrific success with their programs. She would tell me that she couldn't afford it. If only she could join a gym and hire a personal trainer—but again, she couldn't afford it.

As she got older, her knees began to give her trouble and her hip began paining her. Later, she developed high blood pressure and Type 2 diabetes. It was tough to watch because she was sincere in her earnest desire to change, but she needed a support system and couldn't seem to find the extra money for any of the things she knew would work.

Her daughter was overweight like she was and at age 15 developed diabetes and high blood pressure; furthermore, she was being seen by a cardiologist because they were concerned she had developed a heart condition. My friend was devastated. She loved her daughter deeply and felt responsible for her medical problems. Determined not to allow her daughter to regress further, she *found* the money for her daughter and herself to join Weight Watchers. She also enrolled them at a gym in her area. She began getting up at 5:00 A.M. and going to the gym before school and work. They both began to eat better and motivated one another. My friend no longer takes medication for her diabetes or hypertension; neither does her daughter. They have collectively lost 170 pounds and are not stopping.

This story is interesting to me because I am amazed how quickly my friend seemed to find the money when she feared her daughter's prognosis was bleak. This same woman for years spoke of her dreams of going to the gym and joining a weight loss program, but she said over and over she could not afford to do so. She even told me she could not afford to eat healthy. I believe she really believed that; I don't think for a moment that she was using her lack of finances as an excuse. But what is remarkable is how—without a new job, new husband, winning the lottery, or other life-altering episode—she was able to make her daughter's health a priority and the money followed.

My friend's story is not unique. People make choices like that all the time. We say we cannot afford to invest in ourselves. We cannot afford the class, the conference, the books, the memberships—the list goes on and on. But the truth is we simply are not a priority in our own lives, because if we were we would find the money!

I want you to imagine going to the bank today and giving the teller $10,000. Imagine going back in two years and realizing you hadn't gained one penny in interest. What would you think of the bank? I'm pretty certain you'd take your money out of that bank. You would never expect to *invest* in a bank and then get back exactly what you gave them. If you want your life to yield more, you have to be willing to invest in your life. And the truth is, it's not possible to get back exactly what you give. Banks may fail, markets may drop, but if you invest in *you*, you will get a greater return.

I'm sure there are a host of classes you could benefit from, but it will require your investment. Perhaps you need to have your teeth fixed to make *you* more marketable; it will require your investment. Maybe you need to upgrade your wardrobe, invest in a weight loss program, or maybe pay the fees to become part of that business or trade group. Go ahead and pay the price now, because ultimately, you will pay the price one way or the other, either on the front end or the back end. If you invest in your health by eating better and losing weight, you pay less on medication, doctor's visits, and days out of work. Paying the cost to return to school will increase your earning power by at least $25,000.

I challenge you to redirect your thinking. Rather than asking yourself if you can afford the price, write down the price and ask if you have more value than the dollar figure. For example, if you need $3,000 to have your teeth fixed, you have to complete this sentence, "I, _____, deem that I am worth $_____." What amount goes in the blank? Are you worth $3,000? When you write down the figure, the amount, you discover it looks ludicrous to suggest you may not be worth "X" dollars. My friend who found money to invest in her daughter's health never considered that her daughter wasn't worth the price.

After many years of saying with my mouth, "I am worth it!" yet living a contrary truth, I have come to the conclusion that I do not possess enough money to equal the value of my life and the value of my future success. I am worth far more than I could earn or borrow, and so are you. You have to begin to live a life that supports that very truth. The truth of what you believe is found in your check register and your bank statements. I can surmise what you value based on where you spend your money. I can further surmise what your priorities are by where you invest your time, your talent, and your financial resources. If you are going to re-write your success story, your name must be on the top of your list of priorities.

> *You cannot change what you*
> *are willing to tolerate.*

Chapter 10

Pruning Your Life

To enjoy the beautiful garden of your
life, regular pruning is necessary.

WHEN WE THINK OF THE WORD *PRUNE*, WE GENERALLY think of plants, bushes, or other vegetation. The Encarta Dictionary defines *prune* as "to cut away to encourage fuller growth; remove whatever is unwanted or unnecessary." During a pivotal change, we all have to examine our lives and consider what we are willing to cut away to encourage fuller growth. Let's further examine the concept of pruning for a moment.

The four reasons we cut away and prune our plants:

- Train the plant which way it should grow

- Maintain plant health

- Improve quality of flowers, foliage, and stems

- Restrict overgrowth

The first reason to prune is for the sake of training. Training the way we should grow is an arduous feat if we are beginning this in the latter part of our lives. The older we become, the more difficult we are to train. You can positively guess someone's age by how quickly they adapt to change and how willing they are to learn a new process.

Every time there is a Windows™ upgrade, part of me inside groans and wonders, *Why do we have to change it again?* My internal complaint merely magnifies my age. There are things I have had to cut out of my life because they hindered me from growing in the right direction. And just like accepting an upgrade application, my pruning didn't come without internal groaning.

Nearly twenty years ago, I found myself a new inspirational and professional speaker surrounded by an influential group who took pleasure in misspeaking, slang, and fangled language. Much of it was funny, and the few who spoke on stage seemed to capture me with their seamless delivery and humorous punch lines. For their listening audience, this poorly-structured language was welcomed and celebrated; however, my place in the professional speaking community would not allow such disdain for the English language.

Day by day, I was becoming more influenced by a few people who I admired and emulated. I had to consciously tell myself not to use slang or broken English. I found it to be quite difficult until I removed myself from the environment and the people. I identified a few women whom I admired and slowly began challenging myself, my language, and my delivery to meet the standard of the women I now pursued.

Cutting off those relationships which had a "dumbing-down" effect on speech was necessary in order for me to grow for the professional audience I desired. I had to limit my exposure because the poor habits of others were becoming my own poor habits. Cutting unnecessary relationships for the sake of your growth in the right direction is a necessity.

The second reason for pruning is to maintain health. There are simply some things in your life you need to rid yourself of for the sake of your health. Frankly, you need to be healthy to take on the height of success you desire. Your health may require that you stop smoking or drinking alcohol, that you exercise or maybe sleep more.

I have to force myself to go to sleep—not because I'm not tired, but because I am just busy in my mind. I spent years sleeping with the television on and realized it was a hindrance to my sleep and my productivity. It wasn't easy. I liked the background noise, distraction, and lack of focus but in the end that is what my life looked like—noise, distraction, and lack of focus. Consider your health and be willing to prune what is necessary to ensure you are healthy enough to be the successful person you desire to be.

The third reason for pruning is to improve the quality of the fruit or foliage. All of us bear fruit from our lives. Our children are our fruit, what we make with our hands is our fruit, and what we produce in the way of work is our fruit. I realized being around lazy people made me lazy—a lazy mom, a lazy wife, and a lazy worker.

I want quality from my life; therefore, I want to be around people who promote quality. I have a friend who is an incredible housekeeper. When she comes to my house, she's always telling what I need to do differently or what I could be cleaning better, and she may organize my cabinets without my permission while sipping coffee. Many people would be offended by her behavior, but I love it. She teaches and challenges me to be better in this area and thus helps me produce good fruit as a homemaker. I have friends who are incredible mothers who challenge me in the same way to be a better mother. The same is true professionally, spiritually, and every other area in my life. Well, not quite. I don't know any exercise gurus; thus, I lack the desire to work out! Consider what kind of relationships you need to prune in order to produce the kind of beautiful fruit you want.

The fourth reason for pruning is to restrict overgrowth. I have a crape myrtle bush outside of my kitchen window. It was just a wee bitty bush when my husband planted it. Every year that bush grows about 20 feet. It annoys me, it blocks my view, it loses its shape and provides cover for the lizards and other pests I try to avoid. Every year we have to prune the tree or it will completely take over.

There are things in your life that seem to have lives of their own. Like that crape myrtle bush of mine, they are blocking your view. Too much television will hinder you from witnessing your own vision. Reality shows, soap operas—they just take you over and rob you of your own vision. There are things in your life right now that are probably blocking your view—hindering you from seeing clearly and witnessing your vision. Cut them out of your life.

I was once a part of a volunteer effort which seemed more like a coffee klatch. The more coffee they served, the more complaining took place; useless projects were created and little got done. I found my time wasted, and I was becoming emotionally drained at the meetings. Like my crape myrtle, the meetings would lose their perspective and provide a hangout for all kinds of pests. I had to cut it out of my life.

I hope you will do the tough work of cutting out the unnecessary things that are a hindrance to your growth and your vision.

> *Individually, we are one drop. Together, we are an ocean.* —RYUNOSUKE SATORO

Chapter 11

TAKES A COMMUNITY

When I am talking about "It Takes a Village," I'm obviously not talking just about or even primarily about geographical villages any longer, but about the network of relationships and values that do connect us and binds us together. —HILLARY RODHAM CLINTON

I BEGAN WORKING WHEN I WAS 14 YEARS OLD. I PURCHASED my own soap, deodorant, and feminine products. I paid for my hair to be cut and maintained. When I grew older and played sports, had class pictures, or needed funds for any other extracurricular activities, it was at my own expense. When I was just 12, my foster mother made me pay for the hand-me-downs others gave to me. This independent push certainly made me self-reliant, but it also compromised my respect for community support.

One of the most humbling moments in my life was when I came to realize that I could not go it alone. Not just that, but I was not created to go it alone. There is connectivity in the human species that is undeniably innate to our being. From the moment we breathe our first breath of life, we need the contact of other humans to assure the success of our emotional and physical development. As toddlers develop and become independent, they still have need of help. As "independent" adults, we still need support.

Years later, I proudly boasted of my independent streak and need of no one for support of any kind. How naïve I was. It simply is not possible to journey through life without the help of others. There is a balance to need and neediness. We must all recognize our individual strengths, the qualities that set us apart from others, and our talents which are designed to sustain us. Yet still we are part of the human race—we are not superheroes possessing super powers. We need the help of others.

Help takes many forms—introductions, financial favors, domestic help, child care, administrative support, professional expertise, and emergency care. Your needs may permeate outside of the brief offerings here, but I want to expound on taking advantage of these few for your immediate benefit.

INTRODUCTIONS

Most business success happens as a result of a relationship—a real estate deal, a new job opening, a contract opportunity. When you have an inside alliance, you have an edge or an advantage. Meeting the right person can help you gain the edge. Take a look at the people you know and ask yourself, "Who do they know?" Do they know a good attorney, employer, investor, or publisher? After you discover who you know, begin to ask for the introduction. Invite them to lunch or coffee or ask for permission to simply visit their contact at their office. Take advantage of your circle of influence and grow it.

FINANCIAL FAVORS

You may not have enough money, your friends may not have enough money, but perhaps if you take a list of everyone you know and ask for just a little, it may in fact be more than enough. Another option is to ask for a loan. Make certain you truly have the ability to repay; you don't want to lose a friendship over money. A friend may be more forgiving of your previous financial missteps than a bank.

DOMESTIC HELP

When you are in the midst of undertaking a big project, your domestic responsibilities can become overwhelming and all-consuming. Meals don't get made magically, children are not bathed alone, and laundry doesn't dance into the washing machine. And just when you thought you got ahead of the game, one more uniform needs to be ironed.

Make a decision to solicit whatever help you can. Perhaps you can get someone to clean your bathrooms once a week or pick up prepared meals from one of the new trendy meal preparation salons. If finances won't permit such luxuries, prepare a schedule and stick to it. Ask friends or family to assist you where they can and don't forget to get your children involved. Just 30 minutes a day of free time can make a big difference. Have your spouse bathe the children and put them to bed. Or start a meal swap—you commit to make and share a number of meals each month with another family and they do the same. It will free you up several days each month. Get creative, do whatever it takes, and remember—dishes have a way of re-piling each day. If you skip a day the world won't end, but if you do them you may get to the end of your "to do" list and move closer to your dream.

CHILDCARE

Ask a family member or friend if they can keep your children on specific days of the month. Return the favor and commit to a number of days. You will be surprised at the amount of progress you can make without little people asking questions and needing snacks and attention.

ADMINISTRATIVE SUPPORT

Sometimes you may discover you need someone to write, edit, maintain a calendar, or perhaps do research for you. Identify someone who possesses the administrative skills you like and barter your talents. If you don't have an available friend, consider utilizing a virtual assistant. You can obtain the administrative support you need at a super low hourly rate.

PROFESSIONAL EXPERTISE

Don't be afraid to ask those you know, even neighbors, for their professional advice or expertise. It's good to have a professional you can just run a concept or problem by without making the commitment to services. If you eventually contract with a professional, you may have the benefit of doing so with someone you already know and trust.

EMERGENCY CARE

Whether a flood, divorce, or job loss, there may come a time when you need some emergency assistance. Don't make a bad situation worse by failing to ask for help. I have a friend, Cyndy, who knew I needed some help at one time. Not only did she come to my aid, but she discussed my need with others anonymously and other women pitched in to help.

People like to feel they are contributing or participating in something bigger than themselves. Your next chapter is that next big thing. Don't deny yourself and others the joy of contributing to the evolution of your new success.

> *You will never be promoted until*
> *you have become over-qualified*
> *for your present assignment.*

Chapter 12

BECOME AN EXPERT

I am always doing that which I cannot do, in order
that I may learn how to do it. —PABLO PICASSO

NO MATTER WHAT YOUR AREA OF INTEREST, IN ORDER FOR you to realize success, you must first become an expert. People are compensated based on the knowledge they acquire and maintain. There is a reason why people with advanced degrees make more money than those without—advanced knowledge.

Technology has made the process of continual learning so much easier. You should take advantage of the plethora of information available right at your fingertips. Read, study, learn, and contribute. Begin to comment on blogs of experts you admire, or better yet begin your own blog. There are various blogs out there for free where you can disseminate your ideas to a broader audience. Blog radio is also an option which allows you the ability to garner a listening audience. Again, the services are free.

It is important that you are continually challenged to learn; therefore, committing to media forms like blogs and the like allows you the opportunity to share your expertise while forcing you to sharpen your skills and broaden your understanding of your topic. Commit a specific time each day when you read about new things concerning your discipline or perhaps set aside time to visit a location which will further your knowledge of the topic.

I had a friend who divorced her lawyer husband. There came a time when he manipulated the child support which she desperately depended on. Unable to afford an attorney, she began to go to the law library and look up legal precedents whereby she could file a motion. She did so, and to her ex-husband's surprise was granted what she requested. Her diligence had paid off. Yours will too.

Picasso's quote at the beginning of this chapter is well-suited—do that which you cannot so you can learn how to do it. In the end, you will be judged by what you know and what people think you know.

> *The season changes each quarter,*
> *which is comforting; if you missed your*
> *favorite, it'll come around again.*

Chapter 13

JUST A SEASON

Under a blanket of snow, the crimson splendor
of the American Spirit Rose is hidden until
Spring, when the covers are lifted up and
the sun envelopes its face—what beauty.

I REMEMBER BEING A YOUNG GIRL, LOOKING OUT OF MY window at the white blanket of snow, and wondering, *When will summer come?* What was once anticipated with glee—the snow, snowmen, Christmas, igloos, and the like—now was a dirty, useless nuisance. And the wait—it was endless. Or at least it felt that way.

Enduring an unpleasant season in life can feel the same—like endless torture with no expiration date. No matter how many times people tell you, "It will get better...eventually," it doesn't seem to matter. At the moment of your darkest hour, the blackness can seem eternal. But, intellectually, we know that is not true. It simply is not eternal.

Like the winter season which seems to immobilize people, send animals into hibernation, kill beautiful flowers, and freeze everything in sight, our personal life season too may immobilize us, cause us to want to sleep through it, kill our beauty, and freeze our progress. Remember, it is just a season. Eventually, the sun will shine with blazing force, melt the frozen mass, and uncover life—renewed life.

We were not created like bears with the ability to simply sleep months at a time with no food, water, or exercise. So if you find yourself falling into bear behavior, this is your wake-up call. Wake up, shake it off! What will encourage you through your difficult season? The knowledge that a new one awaits you; now plan for the new season.

It's a little like that department store visit you take at the beginning of March while it is still freezing outside. They begin displaying the swimsuits, shorts, t-shirts. Grills begin to go on sale; weekly sales flyers showcase patio furniture. What does all of this visual marketing do? It gets you thinking, investing, and planning for what's to come. It changes your mood; it reshapes your realm of possibilities. You begin imagining maybe you'll travel somewhere exotic or perhaps take a family trip. No matter the depth of your imagination, your future looks different from your present.

So mimic the marketing strategy of the stores and begin looking at something new. Start displaying things around your home that support the season you're waiting for. Awaken your senses to the climate around the corner. Magazine pictures or whatever paraphernalia evoke the sense of change you desperately need should be displayed on your refrigerator, mirrors, and closet doors. Assess your wardrobe and begin to pull out the outfits you'll wear during your new season.

Make sure you spend more time talking about your new season than the one you're in. Children know how to do this well. They can begin talking about Christmas time in September. My girls plan their next birthday the day after their last one. It stirs excitement within. It makes you hopeful and takes your thoughts off of the here and now, if but for a moment.

If you find yourself in a place where you feel immobile and unable to motivate yourself, you may need to solicit the support of your doctor. Don't allow yourself to fall into a slump without seeking the help you need. It is not an admission of weakness but an acknowledgment of love for yourself, your family, and your future.

> *Silence doesn't talk back and*
> *cannot be misquoted.*

Chapter 14

QUIET TIME, QUIET WORLD

I lived in solitude in the country and noticed
how the monotony of a quiet life stimulates
the creative mind. —ALBERT EINSTEIN

WHILE YOU THRUST TOWARD YOUR NEW STORY, CRE-
ative ideas, strategic planning, and the opportunity to simply
dream are essential. I am among those rare women who do not relish
the idea of having regular massages. I can't seem to factor in the time
or usefulness of a manicure, and I find myself wondering how long it
will take the technician to complete this "relaxing" experience.

Long before I had children, my husband would give me certifi-
cates for a day at the spa for Valentine's Day. One year, I donated
nearly $800 in gift certificates to my daughter's school for various
fund raisers. *It simply is not my thing,* I thought.

Following an emotionally difficult experience in my marriage, I visited my uncle Norman in Minnesota. I had never been to Minnesota and was taken aback by its quiet beauty in the spring. I hadn't been on an airplane ride alone for quite some time, and with notebook in hand I began writing ferociously with great ease. My writing continued to flow as I lay in my bed on the second floor of my uncle's home in complete silence as he and his wife worked. I slept lazily at times, dozing off between pages. As a woman who is quite critical of her own work, once I arrived home I was surprised at how compelling my writing was. It was fluid, riveting, and heartfelt.

If I had tried with everything within me, I would not have been able to produce that quality of writing at home, in my space, amidst my family and my crisis. As smart as I believed I was, I never understood the power of solitude. I confused relaxing activities with active relaxing in a quiet environment. Knowing this now, I understand the value of breaking away, even for a day, to nurture creativity and productivity.

You may not have the means to take a trip, but your local park can provide the quiet nature you need to facilitate your progress. Look around your world and examine what is available to you. Be willing to try numerous geographical locations. Like me, you may be surprised at what stirs your imagination.

Finally, don't sabotage your potential by riddling yourself with guilt at your desire, your need, to break away. "I should be with my kids," "I should be cleaning the house," "I should be...." You will be a better mom, homemaker, employee, wife, and friend if you allow your creativity to have an outlet and your talents to have a landing strip with opportunities to flourish.

> *The root word of negative is to negate. It means to invalidate something; so when you choose negativity, you invalidate whatever you're working on: your health, your wealth, your relationships.*

Chapter 15

REMOVING NEGATIVITY

What we focus on, we empower and enlarge. Good multiplies when focused upon. Negativity multiplies when focused upon. The choice is ours: Which do we want more of? —JULIA CAMERON

I WAS STARTLED TO DISCOVER THAT I KNEW A PERSON WHO was unfaithful to her spouse and was attempting to reconcile, yet seemed addicted to the television program *Cheaters*, which is a reality-based show that catches adulterous spouses and confronts them. Why would you engage in a visual depiction of something perfectly opposite of what you say you want? She couldn't find anything wrong with this negative viewing and yet lacked the confidence to believe it was possible for her to have a faithful, monogamous relationship. She couldn't seem to see the correlation between the television program and her lack of confidence in her marriage.

Everything in our life adds or subtracts. Words can add or subtract. Our experiences can add or subtract. And people can add or subtract from your life. Negativity is a single function instrument; it merely subtracts, never adds. Negativity subtracts from your life, your vision, your purpose, and your finances. It sucks your energy, enthusiasm, and hope.

Have you ever been in a terrific mood or really excited about something and then you come around someone who seems to suck the joy right out of your soul? Or maybe you've watched a television show that just brought you down, nearly depressed you. That emptiness you feel at the end of experiencing such a person or program slows you down and strips you of your vigor.

You have to take inventory of your life. Are there people and/or things that project negative energy? Are there people who are trying to convince you that you are going to fail? That your efforts won't work? That you're being silly for trying? What about the things you're listening to on the radio or watching on television? Are they adding to or subtracting from your dream? Do the people in your life and things you surround yourself with push you closer to your dream or pull you further away from it?

You have to make a decision to divorce yourself from whatever is holding you back. Divorce is a final event which occurs when harmony cannot be maintained. There are probably people who have compromised your confidence, harmony, and peace. When you identify who they are, divorce them. You may not even want to contend with the emotional turmoil of discussing it with the person. If you're not up to the task, just continue to let them know that you are unavailable or truly busy working on a project. Am I telling you to avoid them? Yes. This is about your success story. It's about the preservation of your dream. You do whatever it takes. Whatever is necessary.

Finally, divorce the negative imagery. You cannot watch everything. I know we think that because we're grown-ups we are capable of handling serious material on film. We are not. Feeding your mind with victimization, failure, and trauma will only increase your belief in the same.

As the quote at the beginning of this chapter states, you enlarge or make greater whatever you give your focus and attention. If you starve or neglect an area in your life, you will decrease it or make it small. What giant will you feed today?

> *If you can change the way a man thinks*
> *you can change the way he lives.*

C h a p t e r   1 6

CREATE A WINNING MIND

Our life is what our thoughts make it. A man
will find that as he alters his thoughts toward
things and other people, things and other people
will alter toward him. —JAMES ALLEN

IF YOU CAN CHANGE THE WAY YOU THINK, YOU CAN CHANGE
the way you live. If you want to transform your life, you have to
renew your mind. The truth is, you can redo the thing you've had
your whole life—your mind. This is an important and positive refer-
ence because many of us may think, *I've always thought this way,* or
My whole family thinks this way. To *redo* suggests that we are able to
convert old thoughts and make new ones, and as a result of all of that
we are transformed. Transformed into what, you ask? Whatever your
new mind says you desire to be.

Hopefully by the time you are reading this section, you've already begun changing your mind about your possibilities, your future, and your success. The way you think will be your ace to assure you are steadfast until the very end.

I spent years as a young woman hovering at a size 16, nearing an 18. I remember losing a significant amount of weight and being forced to go clothes shopping. I remember the store: Tempo Fashions at the Worcester Center. It seems just like yesterday; I can even recall the pants I was trying on. They had a checkerboard pattern and they were "baggies," which were the craze back then in the mid-eighties. I reached for my size 16, hoping that because they were "baggy" I could avoid going up a size. To my amazement, they fell to the floor. I dressed and went back out to the small store and picked up the 14. Same result. The next time I picked up a 12 and 10. Both sizes were abundantly too large. I recall just staring in the mirror, stunned. How could this be? How had my body melted away without my knowledge? Clearly flipping the waist of my pants couldn't mean I was this small. My fitting room experience continued until I finally put on a comfortable size 4.

What I discovered that day is that although I had experienced significant weight loss success, I had become so accustomed to being overweight that I couldn't wrap my mind around the concept that I had won. The race was over. I had the mind of that young woman who repeatedly failed at weight loss, so I couldn't even recognize what the whole world could. I had lost the weight and had a body I could barely believe was my own.

You have to work diligently at possessing a winning mind—a mind which understands you are not a failure until you succumb to the impossibility of ever winning. A mind that doesn't notice the other people around you who have made it to their finish line already. A mind that is not overtaken by the lack of money, support, or agreement.

So how will you renew your mind? By changing your thoughts. We've already covered negativity, and rejecting negative thoughts seems quite cliché. However, it's not good enough to simply reject negative thoughts; you have to also put in positive thoughts. You have to deposit words, sequences, and thoughts which support your winning endeavors. If left to itself the mind will default to negative, so you have to work daily to support your success.

I am presently overcoming a chronic health ailment. I am very careful of the things which I watch on television. Although the story lines are intriguing, I cannot indulge in medical television dramas. The continued visuals of sick and dying people, trauma, and serious diseases rob me of my confidence and belief that I can truly be healed of the disease. Instead, I consistently ponder words which support miracles, restoration, and healing. I surround myself with articles and topics which promote faith, confidence, and assurance concerning my continued health. As a result of my discipline to renew my mind in this area, it's nearly impossible for me to believe that my future will be riddled with sickness or calamity.

My positive and affirming messages are primarily taken from the Bible. It is the foundation of just about everything I believe. Yours may be another source. No matter—find a few life principles for which you can stand. Develop a response to your losing mindset and be quick to respond. "Respond to myself?" you may be asking, and the answer is yes, to yourself. You possess the loudest mouth you'll ever hear, which is right there in your head. Don't let losing thoughts linger.

Here's an exercise you can try. Begin singing the ABC song. Once you get going, begin counting by tens. Now what happens to the

ABC song? Once you begin another thought, like counting by tens, you have to cease the previous song, ABC. You can use this exercise with just about any scenario.

Winning in any sporting event or life endeavor comes only through consistent and diligent training. You don't make it through your first marathon having only run around the block once. You've spent a whole life training the mind you have now. It won't take you a lifetime to renew it, but understand that it will be a bit more difficult than a walk around the block.

Treat your mind as a gate. Only allow those things that support your success to enter. Close, cut off, and separate from all other messages and words which are contrary to what you have committed to have. Your mind is fragile, the possibilities it holds are endless, its ability to turn ideas into action is sure. For this reason, you must handle it with care. Put your mind on a winning path and the rest of your life will follow.

> *It's easy to make a buck; it's tougher to make a difference.* —TOM BROKAW

Chapter 17

VOLUNTEER FOR WHAT YOU WANT

The highest reward for a person's work is not what they get for it, but what they become because of it.

I HEARD SOMEONE SAY, "VOLUNTEERS ARE SELDOM PAID; NOT because they are worthless, but because they are priceless." And may I say the experience you gain from volunteering is also priceless. I have demonstrated most of my talents and skills while freely giving them away to others or organizations. In a study sponsored by Comcast Foundation, 83 percent of women who volunteer report they acquired, improved, or developed their leadership skills due to volunteer participation, while 78 percent saw improvement in communication skills.

I first began speaking as an orientation trainer for a nonprofit. I could not have imagined that developing that skill would place me in front of thousands. But it began in front of a small group within a nonprofit organization. What was my pay for those services? Zero. What was the value of discovering and honing one of my greatest skills? Priceless.

My skills for writing, speaking, training, graphic design, organization, and leadership all were acquired and cultivated while volunteering at a nonprofit. Imagine what you could learn, what you could perfect, while volunteering.

I recommend you put volunteering in your arsenal to boost your resume, business plan, family plan, and life plan. The opportunities are countless. Begin to ask yourself who you want to be, what you need to learn, what type of people or environment would benefit from your desires. Then begin to list at least ten organizations where you could serve to meet that need.

I recommended a client of mine to volunteer at Girls, Inc. and speak to a group of young girls at an annual conference. My client had no prior experience speaking but felt comforted by the idea that she would be speaking to girls and the assignment seemed to resonate with a passion she had for at-risk youth. The organization provided an orientation and gave specific topics and notes to the facilitators detailing what they would say. My client had a terrific and successful meeting. She was quite proud of herself and committed to serve on a regular basis. This one small act opened doors of opportunity for her and stretched her to add speaking to her arsenal of talent.

If you need to sharpen your fundraising skills, volunteer that. If you want to learn more about homebuilding, volunteer at Habitat for Humanity. If you want to get involved in television, volunteer at your local PBS station. Do your best to identify an organization which you believe in or one which you'd even like to work for.

I presently have a client who desires to develop a girl's summer camp which will instill confidence, positive imagery, and higher self-esteem in the young girls who will attend. She recently volunteered at a summer camp for entrepreneurially-minded youth. Although the camp goals are remarkably different, I wanted her to learn the importance of a sound curriculum and what it takes to maintain the interest of adolescent campers. She was quite excited and learned a great deal, which she'll incorporate into her own program. I imagine she'll become more enthusiastic in pondering her own project after learning from someone who is already doing well what she has yet to do.

Getting a volunteer opportunity isn't as easy as you think. An organization isn't interested in sharing its intellectual capital with someone who is there merely to extract its creative resources. Solicit a volunteer opportunity the same as you would a job. Provide a resume and cover letter expressing your qualifications and your desire to serve. Be sure to learn something about the organization in advance and include a few details in your cover letter. They should be able to see your passion on paper.

If your best selling quality is your appearance, I recommend that you bring your resume and cover letter there in person. If you are best represented on paper, then allow your resume and cover letter to do on paper what you perhaps cannot do in person. Sell *you!*

Make a list of skills you would like to gain from your volunteer experience. Be very specific. It's easy to find yourself in the midst of a needy organization and getting engrossed in their mission and forgetting your own. You want to serve the organization with commitment and excellence; however, remember this is volunteerism with a purpose of its own. Make certain that you are acquiring the skills that are going to benefit you. Again, if you want to learn something about fundraising, being the person who collects clothes from people's houses may not be the answer.

Your volunteer service will help you do the following:

- Beef up your resume with experience

- Provide you with a skill set you need to apply to a personal endeavor or project

- Connect you with people who may serve as mentors, business partners, or friends

- Fill in the gaps of unemployment

- Allow you to intern for what you really want and discover if it is a good fit

So analyze the opportunities and make sure you are volunteering for exactly what you need. You will undoubtedly learn other skills by virtue of being there, but minimally make sure you are acquiring what you volunteered for. Once you've achieved this task, be willing to share the information with others. When someone shares something of value with you and you benefit from it, you have a moral obligation to share it with others.

> *A picture is a snapshot of your history;*
> *vision is a preview of your future.*

Chapter 18

CHANGING YOUR PICTURES

Every artist dips his brush in his own
soul, and paints his own nature into his
pictures. —HENRY WARD BEECHER

THE ENCARTA DICTIONARY DEFINES THE WORD *PICTURE* AS
follows:

1. To imagine or have an image of somebody or something in mind;

2. A vivid image or impression in the mind of how somebody or something looks.

Pictures are still shots of the past or can be imagery of an imagined future. You've heard the saying, "A picture is worth a thousand words." Pictures do, in fact, tell stories. The stories may not necessarily be true, but they are stories nonetheless.

You've seen portraits of families who look so happy together, but later you discover there was significant turmoil and pain. Or perhaps you've seen someone's picture on a social media or dating site. They look young, fit, and attractive, but when you meet them in person you realize things are not always as they seem.

If I looked through your photo albums or through the batches of pictures you possess that haven't quite made it into albums, I'd be able to see a lot about your life, your family, your adventures, your jobs, and your accomplishments. Your album would be riddled with graduations, housewarmings, baby showers, weddings, and ribbon cuttings. The pictures would tell many a story, building year after year. Much of what I saw would be factual, some perhaps fantasy or complete fallacy, but all would be a depiction of where you'd been.

The first definition of the word *picture* is "to imagine or to have an image of somebody or something in mind." I like this description the best because it asserts the idea of imagination—not simply a factual image, but an imagination. So now that I've visited your past by way of your photo album, what do you possess that allows me to visit your future? Where would I find the "one thousand words" describing your next chapter, your future? Imagery, as we've already discussed, is important in making a believer out of you and those around you. It acts as a motivator, stimulator, and fuel to force you to continue reaching for newer and higher heights.

Before my husband and I were married, we would go out on the weekends and look at houses. We would take the floor plans of the houses we visited and put them on the refrigerators in our individual apartments. Once we settled on a house and the financing scrutiny began, we placed the picture of that specific floor plan in our respective apartments and began calling it our house. We imagined what we'd put in each of the rooms. Whose furniture would go where? He would ask me, "You still got the picture up?"

"Of course," I'd answer. We took this process very seriously.

I remember my husband was challenged by the lender because of information concerning his credit. It was an error which actually was a part of his father's credit history, but neither of us knew that at the time. We were not moved one bit. We were so completely fixed on the image we'd been seeing each day that we could not imagine anything other than us living in that house. Of course my husband's credit was corrected and the matter redeemed. Just a few months later we were married and living in the house we had imagined.

Imagery matters. Pictures matter. They help shape your dreams, your hopes, and your expectations. They are the building blocks of what could be and they support what you believe. So what types of pictures surround your home? Are they simply pictures of what is or do you have anything that suggests where you will be going?

People hoping to make it to Paris one day may have posters, photos, or clocks shaped like the Eiffel Tower. Surrounding oneself with imagery reinforces the reality of the inevitability. So prepare for your inevitability by creating your future on paper, corkboard, or poster board. Many people who undertake projects like this use names like *dream board*, but a dream is a goal without a date or definite ending. There will be a definite ending to your chapter, it will come to pass. So instead, I choose to call it a *vision board*. It is something that you've seen with spiritual eyes and now others will see with physical eyes.

Take a trip to your local craft store and pick up the supplies you'll need. You can be as sophisticated or understated as your wallet and your imagination take you. Consider the collage you'll make on your vision board. Consider this a visual summary of your new story, the corresponding cover to your new chapter. What would that look like?

Begin by giving it a title: Talk Show Host, Married and Marvelous, Renowned Baker, Weight Loss Success Story! Make sure your picture is on the collage somewhere. You may want to take a new picture with your winning smile or perhaps styled the way you will look when you complete your goal. Then surround your pictures with magazine cutouts and photos that reflect all of what your fulfilled goal will encompass. The building, the people, the furnishings, the home, the business name, etc. You should be able to see every aspect of your dream featured on your vision board.

Once completed, be sure to place your vision board prominently where it can be regularly seen. You want to view it each day until it becomes a familiar image. When visitors drop by and ask about your display, be sure to explain your mission, your dream, and your goal. Ask them if they think there should be something else on your collage that you are missing. Engaging others will only add fuel to your passion and will also provide another layer of accountability. Invite your friends to support and encourage you as well as rebuke you when your actions are contrary to the dream you've displayed.

As you begin to realize milestones on your display, circle them and write things like "yeah" or "did it" or "done." You and everyone else who walks by that display will see your progress. Their celebration and your own pride will empower you to be diligent until it all is realized.

> *Successful people turn everyone who can help them into "sometime" mentors!* —JOHN CROSBY

Chapter 19

FIND A MENTOR

A mentor is someone whose hindsight can become your foresight. —AUTHOR UNKNOWN

MENTORS ARE NOT PERFECT PEOPLE. THEY ARE PEOPLE who have experienced life and are capable of sharing their knowledge and wisdom with you. They may be older or younger; no matter what age, they have the ability to grow your dream. I recommend you find a mentor of the same sex as that way you will not encounter any unnecessary or potential conflicts. The following examples are from my experiences, although men can certainly realize the need for good mentors as well.

Mentors are seasoned and have walked where you presently journey. They have experienced both success and failure and are not afraid to share both with you. Mentors will save you years of mistakes, loss, and failure. You may make it to the end of your dream without a mentor, but you will have suffered unnecessary hardship without one.

I remember getting my footing in my outreach. Right away I had a few women who believed in me and graciously offered financial support to enable me to do what I desired for women. I recall reaching out for help to the only people I knew who had done what I was embarking upon. To my disappointment, they did not respond at all. I felt a bit bewildered because I had never hosted a conference, been on television or radio, or printed a magazine, and yet these were all projects I was preparing to produce.

I forged ahead without any counsel, and although my efforts seemed successful on the surface, I spent a lot of money on services I recognize today were unfruitful. I repeated many of the same mistakes again and again as I continued on the path of hosting women's conferences and seminars. The polish and excellence of my presentations covered up a multitude of my mistakes. I wished I had someone in my life who was willing to share their experience and not feel threatened that I just might do something wonderful with it.

Today, I try my best to be honest with other women who are traveling where I've already journeyed. I am passionate about saving others from financial loss and failure. I am to others what I wish someone had been to me. Much of my passion as a life and recovery coach is rooted in frustration from a lack of support and guidance during my own evolution as a conference speaker and host.

I have many mentors in my life now. My husband once inquired why I am connected to a certain woman. Her professional aptitude was bleak, her network of influence non-existent, and her marriage needed life support. Well, I found her ability to manage her finances and her household remarkable. She knew how to make her food stretch and her dollars go further and was capable of fixing just about anything you could imagine. I recognized she had skills that I lacked, and although her life wasn't perfect, neither was mine. I am smart enough and mature enough to extract from her exactly what I need and separate her weaknesses from her strengths.

I have another woman who is a spiritual mentor to me. Again, her life is not perfect—she struggles within her marriage and she is not perfectly proud of how she parented her children—but she is a spiritual guide to me and I can trust her confidence and her wisdom. Again, I am able to separate the parts that are not perfect from the parts which are capable of perfecting me.

I have a woman I rely on for parenting advice who has done it incredibly well and a woman who is an outstanding professional coach and conference speaker. It is necessary for you to note that none of these women are capable of being everything to me. Each person plays a unique and important role in providing insight, knowledge, and critique. I humbly accept both rebuke and encouragement from them and do not take their time, talent, or wisdom for granted. I am certain to remind them with gifts, words, and notes how very valuable they are to me.

So how are you going to find a mentor? Identify exactly what you need. Begin to look around at the people you already know and analyze if they possess the quality your desire. Remember, they don't have to be everything—just something. If the mentor you need is not in your life, seek out women in your community, your church, or your school who possess the skills and knowledge that you need.

If you don't already have a personal relationship with a mentor, you should recognize that people's time is their rarest and probably most valuable commodity. As such, don't assume that your potential mentor will be all giddy about spending extra time with you. Your relationship should appear as an exchange of sorts. For example, perhaps you can volunteer to assist your mentor with tedious or mundane projects that they don't have the time or resources to complete themselves. Perhaps the time you volunteer is bartered for a consult or coaching session, hour for hour.

Or perhaps you have the finances to pay for your mentor's time. You can invite her to lunch or dinner or pay for an organizational event that you both have interest in. Consider paying for an hour of her time—at least offer. Depending on her degree of value, I would offer between $150 and $1,500 for the hour. You may find the price range vast and increasingly pricey, however, a stay-at-home mom who teaches you how to homeschool, a marriage therapist, or the CEO of a company have very different requirements. Offering to pay someone demonstrates your respect for their talent and time. I highly recommend you do this, particularly for people with whom you have no relationship.

Whether you volunteer or pay a consulting fee, please know that your investment will not compare to the invaluable information you will retrieve from your mentor. Consider yourself fortunate when you identify a person or people who will lend themselves to developing your dream.

I hope when you have realized your dream you will remember how it felt to have someone to give you relevant advice and encouragement. I further hope you will pay it forward and find another woman to mentor and encourage. Your return on the investment will definitely be much greater than your initial offering.

> *If you cannot be a poet, be the*
> *poem.* —DAVID CARRADINE

Chapter 20

STANDING OUT

Stop trying to fit in when you were born to stand
out! —FROM THE FILM, *What a Girl Wants*

MY DAUGHTER NOELLE DECIDED THAT SHE WANTED TO
see *The Princess and the Frog.* Although she was excited, she
couldn't understand why so many adults were making such a fuss over
the movie. All this talk about Disney's first African American princess—what was wrong with them? After all, Noelle thought she was
Disney's first African American princess. Really she did. She never
saw an outfit that wouldn't be fashioned just right with princess high
heels. Never was there a school uniform, pajamas, or swimsuit that
wouldn't be more dazzling with princess diamonds and rubies. And
what's the point of a head if not to hold a tiara in place?

So you can imagine premiere night at my house. Noelle invited
her friends over to properly dress for this important night. You see,

she's been my daughter for several years, so when she says things like, "Can I wear this tutu over my jeans to the mall?" I think, *Of course; perhaps someone else will be dressed like that at the mall.*

When she asked to wear her Cinderella dress in July when we went bowling, I said, "Sure, knock yourself out." *Maybe there will be another little girl there with a costume on.* So I wasn't surprised that on this night of nights, the movie premiere, Noelle wanted to be dazzling.

She and her girlfriends gathered at my house and, of course, dressed the part. Her little friend Madeline didn't have a costume, so of course we had a trunk holding at least 50 ensembles to choose from, along with many tiaras, jewelry, shoes, and the like. Her friend Tye came with a Princess Tiana gown, tiara, and high-heeled shoes.

So off we went to the movies. People stared and smiled and waved. *What a sight*, they thought. And to my surprise no one, not one, was dressed in costume. I thought for sure this would be the time when the room would be crawling with Princess "wannabees." But no, just as before, we stood alone—us in our costumes—as others stared. This, after all, was Noelle's brand—her stand-out quality and hers alone. It is what makes her special and yet predictable. It is what she is excused for but yet is unapologetic. Noelle stands out!

Unlike most fairytales, the tale of my seven-year-old standout princess is one we can learn much from today. Identifying and then embracing our standout quality will give us the edge, the advantage we need to excel in our endeavors, whether we want a better marriage, to be a better parent, or to have a better career.

You may be uncertain of what your standout quality is. I will use the word *brand* to simplify this concept. Imagine one sequined white glove and tell me what entertainer comes to mind. How about suspenders? When you think of a personality who wears suspenders all the time, who would come to mind? What about real estate? Who is the most notable real estate icon you can think of? The answers to these questions are Michael Jackson, Larry King, and Donald Trump, respectively. They have, deliberately or not, created an image in the minds of viewers and readers alike.

Their standout quality or brand is so solidified in our minds that just the mention of a few clothing items has brought two of these men to your mind. The third icon, Donald Trump, renowned as a real estate giant, is not the most successful or even the richest real estate tycoon, but he has branded himself so well that when you mention the words *real estate*, Donald Trump comes to mind.

To stand out means to gain attention, to be noticed, or to be branded. In a world filled with competent, smart professionals, how will you stand out? If you're in a family which needs to be re-branded and set back on track, what remarkable quality do you possess that you can market to your spouse and/or children and remind them of how valuable and irreplaceable you are?

Some know this answer right away, others have to ponder deeply or ask others for their feedback. Whatever tactic you must employ, I encourage you to discover your brand today and get busy marketing *you*.

You may say, "I'm a proficient writer or editor," "I'm a marvelous baker," or, "I am an organization guru." Whatever your brand, make sure the world knows it. It is your job to market yourself.

No matter where you are in the process of your next chapter, take the time to create personal brand cards. These are business cards which, instead of a professional title, offer your life mission statement or your standout quality. For example, I presently have a personal brand card which says:

EVELYN D. WATKINS
Life and Business Recovery Coach
Helping you pick up the pieces and start over again.

As I evolve and my qualities and my skill sets change, I change my statement. I encourage you to do this task today. It will force you to stop calling yourself by your title and instead begin calling yourself by your life mission. The more you begin to say who you are, the more you will believe it and the more you will be requested for your mission rather than your profession.

If by chance your standout quality is something negative, you must do everything necessary to change that today. If you're still unsure what your standout quality is, ask someone—someone honest, not someone who will tell you what you want to hear.

Here are a few summarized final thoughts:

1. Recognize your talents; your talents may be different from what you're known for.

2. Begin a historical success record—thank you notes, emails, or letters from superiors or clients. Get a three-ring binder and begin to build your own success journal.

3. Communicate your value to others.

4. Project confidence.

Your presence should say that you know something that others don't. It's not arrogant; it is certain. Walk into your next opportunity with confidence. If you're not going to stand up and stand out, you might as well sit down.

> *You must have long-range goals to keep you from being frustrated by short-range failures.* —Charles C. Noble

Chapter 21

EMBRACING FAILURE

Life's real failure is when you do not realize how close you were to success when you gave up.

FAILURE IS AN EVENT; IT IS NOT A PERSON. YOUR POTENTIAL success should not be entangled in the possibility of an event but in the possibilities of you—a person. Wise people know how to respond to failure. They understand that events and experiences can become directional tools to discover the right path of success.

How someone manages perceived failure is rooted in how they see themselves. I just completed an application for a television opportunity, and the producer asked the question, "How do you handle failure? How do you behave when you win?"

My answer may sound Pollyanna but it is rooted in what I believe about myself. If, for example, I trained to run a race and lost, I would not feel like a failure; instead, I would celebrate my best effort and realize that someone more qualified, capable, and destined to win actually won. Any other response would be self-sabotage. My approach to loss is the same in every case. Keep in mind, I may feel frustrated if I didn't give my all and lost, but it wouldn't be anger at the loss, instead it would be disappointment in myself for not being better prepared or equipped for the opportunity. A healthy sense of oneself will produce a healthy response to loss.

Successful salespeople say that knowing that fourteen out of fifteen people will say *no* merely inspires them to quickly make their presentations to as many as possible to reach that one person who will accept. Rejection or perceived failure is part of the life cycle of success. The only true way you will know if something will work is if you try. You may try and fail, but then you will have acquired the knowledge of what doesn't work, which is equally as important as what does work.

No matter what the attempt is—online dating, business startup, or marriage—they all have the potential to fall apart and fail. How you face the event will demonstrate not simply what you believe about failure but what you believe about yourself.

Say you have an idea, and you pitch your idea to a bank. They aren't interested in your dream or what you have to say—shake it off and move on. You present a new idea you've been working on to senior staff at work—they're uninterested and unimpressed. Shake it off and move on. Your spouse has told you they are no longer in love with you and they have filed for divorce. Shake it off and move on. The rejection is not a death sentence; it is merely someone's opinion. Make sure you don't allow someone's opinion to define *your* opinion of yourself.

There are things that last long after the event of failure and rejection—your hopes, goals, and dreams. Not everyone will like you, celebrate you, or care one bit about your future. But there is someone out there—it could be one person or many—who needs what you have. Your role must be to continue to develop yourself and nurture your ideas, dreams, and passions. Then, identify *those people* who will appreciate you and your contribution.

Vera Wang was a senior fashion editor for *Vogue* magazine for sixteen years. In 1985, she left *Vogue* after being turned down for the editor-in-chief position. She then joined Ralph Lauren as a design director for two years. In 1990, she opened her own design salon in the Carlyle Hotel in New York that featured her trademark bridal gowns. I don't know what was going through her mind when she was overlooked for the editor-in-chief position. I don't know if she was offended, felt like a failure, or was too busy looking for her next opportunity to ponder it much at all, but I do know that had Vera been given that position at *Vogue*, we may not have the treasure of her beautiful wedding gowns and extensive fashion line. She may have delayed or never tapped into her love of fashion through her own creations.

The wonderful story of Vera Wang is a beautiful depiction of rejection provoking or forcing a new path. It's a little like taking a trip to DC and the airplane experiences terrible turbulence due to storms in the region. Air traffic control denies the pilot permission to land anywhere in the area. They recommend he land in New York where multiple departures are available for the passengers. Imagine everyone on the plane annoyed at how this has interfered with their scheduled plans. On the one hand you're grateful the airline is making a choice for your safety and well-being, but on the other hand your plans are now ruined and you're left having to re-configure your schedule.

Imagine further that there are no flights until the next evening, and you're now stranded in New York City. Are you the person who decides to leave the airport and explore the city you've been forced to stay in until the next night? Or are you the person who we see sleeping in the chair at the airport—miserable, mad, and seemingly lacking control of your present condition?

The person who takes on the city, goes to a show, or enjoys one of New York's restaurants is a person who embraces a failed plan, makes the most of it, and doesn't allow it to define or dictate the rest of their journey.

You may not have control over someone rejecting you, denying your request, falling out of love with you, or writing a bad review about you, but you can control how you respond. You can control how you map out the rest of your journey and what you choose to learn from the experience in the midst of it. You can take on the Big Apple or slouch in a chair thinking about what could have been as it eats at your core.

I choose the Apple.

> *The prophetic certainty of your future*
> *is revealed in your daily routine.*

Chapter 22

COMMIT TO CONSISTENCY

What we hope ever to do with ease, we must learn
first to do with diligence. —SAMUEL JOHNSON

YOUR DAILY HABITS DETERMINE YOUR FUTURE. IF YOU
make a habit of working out each day, you will undoubtedly be
physically fit. If you make a habit of flossing your teeth, you likely will
not suffer from gum disease. Negative habits will produce negative
results in your future. Positive habits will produce positive results in
your future.

The funny thing about a habit is that once it is established, it can
be quite difficult to break. Ask smokers how easy it is to break the
habit. Even with the aid of nicotine patches or medications which
calm the physical addiction, the emotional and psychological addiction is equally if not more difficult to break.

There is a series of humorous television commercials directed at people who desire to quit smoking. It shows a person who is trying to quit smoking and she behaves as though she has never drunk a cup of coffee before. She spills coffee all over herself because she developed a habit of smoking while drinking coffee. They repeat this concept with a person who is seemingly unable to drive without smoking. It is a truly terrific visual depiction of the power of habit. Of course, that image reflects the power of a negative habit. The power which takes over a smoker attempting to quit is the same power which can overtake you as you apply diligence to a positive effort.

Maxwell Maltz has researched the power of habit and has come up with a technique which has been pretty much adapted as a standard tool for success. The essence of the technique is simply to devote 15 minutes a day to the formation of any habit you wish to establish, and consistently continue this effort faithfully for 21 days. By the fourth week, you should have a much more difficult time avoiding your new habit than you would to simply continue doing it.

This technique applies to any form of habit, whether it is a physical practice or a way of perceiving something, such as self-image. The book *Zero Resistance Living* explains how to change your self-image in "the theater of your mind," 15 minutes a day for 21 days.

It will also help to establish the habit if the behavior, such as jogging, is performed at the same time of day every day. Other senses can be utilized to establish the habit. For example, if you want to establish the habit of meditating, you can reinforce the practice by wearing the same clothing, occupying the same location, and assuming the same posture.

The more senses you can involve in the new habit, the more likely it is to become ingrained in the neural pathways. Therefore, even if you're working on your self-image in a mental construct, it's helpful to use all the faculties of your imagination to include sights, sounds, smells, and the senses of feeling and taste to strengthen the image which you come to associate with your new self-image. In other words, make it seem as real as possible.

If you miss a day, just keep going until you've been doing the new behavior for 21 days in a row. Now just because this technique sounds simple doesn't mean that the process is easy. Change is never easy. If it was, everyone would do it and have great habits. Change is difficult. Developing new habits is difficult. But difficult doesn't mean impossible; it means adjustment. You have to adjust your priorities and make yourself, your wellbeing, and your success a priority.

This is a significant challenge. I tell people I coach to pretend they are making the change for a child, aging parent, or anyone else they deeply care for. We can commit for others much easier than we can for ourselves.

Next, commit to small changes at a time. If you are writing a play, commit to perhaps 30 minutes a day to begin. If you are launching a new business but still work full time, find 15 to 30 minutes a day to work on your business plan or sales strategy. Create small, achievable milestones that you can easily complete without overwhelming yourself. No matter how many half-hour infomercials you watch with 30-minute hot body transformations, it doesn't happen in 30 minutes on one day. It is a daily commitment to obtain extraordinary results.

What would I learn about your life by watching your daily habits for a week? Would I witness habits that support your dream or habits that compromise what you say you want? Your calendar, your bank transactions, and your check register are quite revealing of your habits. Make an honest assessment of your present habits. Make a commitment to stop the hindrances and reinforce the small steps you've taken thus far. Write down the commitment and cross out the days on your calendar that you have consistently completed your task or milestone. With every day that passes that you've been consistent, your proud sense of accomplishment will fuel you to continue.

Look at day 22 on your calendar and imagine who your habits will say you can be.

> *Words are only postage stamps delivering*
> *the object for you to unwrap.*

Chapter 23

CHANGING THE CONVERSATION

Watch your thoughts, for they become words. Watch
your words, for they become actions. Watch your
actions, for they become habits. Watch your habits,
for they become character. Watch your character, for
it becomes your destiny. —AUTHOR UNKNOWN

THE REASON I WROTE THE CHAPTER "CREATE A WINNING
Mind" before this one is that I recognize the progression of a
thought. The quote for this chapter so eloquently demonstrates the
evolution of a thought. Thought to word, word to action, action to
habit, habit to character, and character to destiny. How profound.

Because we've already begun developing a winning mind, I hope
you will be able to understand the relevance of watching your words
and changing your conversation to support the life you want. This
can be one of the most difficult tasks we undertake. Not simply

talking positive, but using language that supports the life we are working toward.

So if you believe the quote on the previous page, and your words become your actions, what kind of actions should you anticipate based on the words you speak? When you get frustrated do you say things like, "This is never going to work," or, "My credit is so bad, I know they're never going to give me the money"? Is that really the action you want to follow your words? Failure and rejection? Then why say it?

We are accustomed to saying lots of things we either don't believe or don't want, yet we say them anyway. *I died laughing. He's never going to give me _____! I looked big as a house. She coughed to death. I ate like a pig.* Just empty exaggerations that we really don't actually believe, nor do we want them to happen.

You know that old adage, "Say what you mean and mean what you say"? Well, that is a wonderful mandate to live by. Let's first begin to say what we mean. If you laughed really hard, say that. No need to add death to the laughter. We'll all believe you if you say you laughed hard. If you look fatter than you ever have, say that. No need to compare your body to the size of a house.

Our first task is to discipline our mouths to be thoughtful about even the little things. Let there be integrity in our words. Become speakers who mean what we say.

I remember having great difficulty conceiving my first daughter, Gabrielle. No one was aware of the distress my husband and I faced, particularly when my doctor told me that I was a poor candidate for in vitro fertilization and that he had exhausted all of his options. My husband's eyes were full as the doctor further detailed the results of our tests.

I chose, when I left that day, to not allow my words to be altered based on what we heard. I continued to talk about our future with a child as though he had confirmed a pregnancy. In fact, I went to a baby furniture store with my friend Shirley and put a crib on layaway. At the checkout, the representative asked me a few questions to complete the layaway. When he asked for my due date, I responded, "Due season." He was intrigued and wanted to know what I meant. I told him I wasn't exactly pregnant yet but was making a "faith purchase" for the baby I would eventually have. He was delighted at the concept and asked if I would send him more faith buyers!

It would be three years before I would talk to an associate about my layaway. In fact, when I became pregnant the crib was no longer offered. I had to purchase something else.

My conversation never changed. I didn't lie; I didn't exaggerate; I simply refused to speak contrary to what we were working toward and what I believed I would eventually have. I did not want my words to undermine my efforts. Christian believers call this *faith talk*, new-agers call it "the power of positive speaking." I simply call it the truth. It was my truth. Eventually, I did get the privilege of becoming a mother, and no one around me was aware of our tumultuous season; they didn't know because my words and conversation never wavered.

You have to assess your conversation and honestly judge what people would surmise, because the truth of your life based upon your words. Begin with the small things you say that you don't believe and stop saying them. Stop sabotaging your success and work on becoming a deliberate speaker. Say deliberately what you want rather than what is.

What begins as a deliberate, conscious sentence will soon evolve into a natural conversation. Before you know it, you will converse like the CEO, author, new parent, or senior manager that you are!

> *A toddler marvels at his first steps, knowing he'll soon be able to cruise a whole world by foot. What an ambitious goal!*

Chapter 24

Make a Milestone Out of Your Molehill

One of the secrets of life is to make stepping stones out of stumbling blocks. —Jack Penn

I KNOW WE'VE ALL HEARD THAT SAYING, "DON'T MAKE A mountain out of a molehill." The implication is that we make big things out of very little things. Clearly this adage has a negative connotation, but I would like to use the same exaggeration to move from small things to bigger things.

A coach of any sort understands that champions are not born, they are developed over time. Small measures, small exercises yield large returns. As a life coach, I partner with individuals to conquer small milestones and build on them.

As previously mentioned, success is in the level of detail you set in the milestone. Milestones are created as stepping stones to your goals. The objective is to create small, easy-to-achieve tasks that will bring you closer to your goals until they are actually realized. When working with clients, I ask them a series of questions which will aide in discovering what would be a meaningful milestone to list for completion. I will summarize a few for you below and explain.

1. What was the most recent goal you completed, great or small?

This is an important question because, first, it reminds you that you have successfully completed a goal. Second, it offers us your unique success strategy.

2. Why do you believe you were successful in achieving this goal?

I like people to offer at least three keys to the success of a prior goal. For example, family support, waking up earlier, or cutting back on frivolous spending. Usually clients find at least two answers to their future success in one of their past successes.

3. Describe your most recent unfulfilled goal.

4. Describe three reasons you believe the goal remains unfulfilled.

The three reasons clients list are generally obstacles they've endured for some time and perhaps have become excuses for not moving forward. I usually encourage clients to develop a response to each of the reasons they've listed. Because they've already listed success keys, many of their responses will be found in their prior success.

5. List three things you can begin doing tomorrow to bring you closer to your goal.

The three things they list should be immediately achievable. These are the beginnings of their goals or their milestones. This is just a brief summary of questions asked during an initial assessment for strategic life planning. What is most important is to be true to yourself. There is no sense in saying you're going to begin each day with an hour of meditation if you know you could only last ten minutes. Start with what you know you can do; win, then use that winning power to build on your success.

I remember telling my husband I was going to begin power walking. I did not work out at all at the time and thought walking through my neighborhood would be a good start for a person who was as sedentary as me. He helped me by purchasing some small weights for my strength training. Of course, I invested in a great outfit which would reflect my naturally-sculpted shoulders, arms, and pectorals.

So off I went on my first walk. My new sneakers were the finishing touch to a really polished look. I didn't realize until that moment how hilly my neighborhood was. But I continued. My breath labored, I began sweating, and I didn't have the great attitude I had when I set out. I noticed litter, neighbors' unkempt lawns, and loud children. I couldn't believe I lived there. The longer I walked, the more annoyed I was at everyone and everything. After a while I began to get annoyed with people waving and smiling at me. *Stop staring*, I thought to myself. Finally, my walk had come to an end. I had walked for just over an hour and collapsed on my front steps. My husband was quite proud of my effort. He was just grateful I had finally taken on some form of exercise. "How far did you go?" he asked.

"I don't know, about two or three miles," I said.

"Really? Where did you walk?" I told him how far I had gone, hills and all. "Evelyn, that wasn't even a mile!" he laughed aloud.

I was adamant at my progress and quite perturbed he would challenge my effort. I bustled back in the house, showered, changed, and talked about him under my breath. *The nerve*, I thought to myself. He was just jealous of how quickly I adapted to his world of fitness.

I got in my car after he drove off and reset the odometer to zero. I retraced my steps in the car with the comfort of my air conditioning. I happily smiled and waved to all of those people who annoyed me just moments ago. Making it back to my driveway I looked down at the odometer. I couldn't believe my eyes—half of a mile. A half a mile—how was that possible? The sweat, the heart racing and palpitations for just a half a mile? Well guess what? I didn't go power walking again for four years. You see, I had set an unreasonable goal for a person who led a sedentary lifestyle. So instead of applauding my good start, my great effort, I shamed myself and did nothing further. In the end, my great outfit, new sneakers and sweat meant nothing because it was just one stepping stone to my couch.

Starting with great supplies, a wonderful smile, and a winning attitude will profit you nothing if your expectations and goals do not support your absolute success. Your milestones can indeed become mountains, so choose them wisely.

> *Laughing at yourself beats others to the punch!* —GROUCHO MARX

Chapter 25

YOUR STANDUP COMEDY SHOW

**Laughter is the shock absorber
that eases the blows of life.**

I RECALL ONE DAY WHEN MY FAMILY WAS GATHERED together; we were reminiscing about our youth. My early childhood was riddled with a great deal of abuse which my siblings and I endured and overcame. The memories seem so outrageous today and yet very familiar. We had withstood the physical and verbal assaults with our sound minds intact.

My husband and a few of my sisters' husbands were present as we recounted walking down the hallway with our hands protecting our faces, never walking quite erect when passing my mom. We dramatically replayed the scene in front of one another. We laughed from the pit of our bellies, both at our reenactment and the humiliation of it all—fearing your parent with such sober anguish. Tears filled our eyes as we held our stomachs and rolled with hilarity.

My husband looked on, also with tears in his eyes, but not from laughter. He and the other outsiders were bewildered at our behavior. How could we laugh at such travail? What was wrong with us? My husband excused himself and left the room. The other in-laws drifted away as well. They were gravely uncomfortable and couldn't find the humor in our stories, to which we had become accustomed.

Our experiences were difficult indeed, but we had learned to find the humor even in dark stories. Laughter really is a shock absorber. It softens the hard blows life delivers. Laughter doesn't make a tragedy okay, but it can make revisiting it, correcting it, and rebuilding feel okay.

I can make comedy out of any painful situation imaginable, and I've had plenty. It's not necessary that everyone get it; what is necessary is that you are able to laugh in the midst of your difficult time.

I remember early in my marriage we endured great financial difficulties. I perused our pantry and saw a whole lot of nothing and payday was many days away. We would have to make do with the green beans and bread because it literally was all that we had. I laughed to myself and thought, *Well, I guess we're going to have a fast this week.* When I told my husband we would be fasting this week, he asked what kind of fast it would be. "A green bean fast, of course!" Oh, did we laugh! We really couldn't do much more that week except for endure and laugh.

There are times during your quest for success that you really must see the laugh in everything. It is merely a matter of perception. Dark humor, light humor, juvenile humor, whatever humor you need for the situation you find yourself in—find it and laugh, really laugh loud.

I remember working at the housing authority in Massachusetts in the 1980s. I worked with a woman named Dorothy. She was in her early sixties, nearing retirement, and lived with her sister. The two of them together never expected life to pass so quickly and hadn't quite planned their finances for the early retirement they wanted. She would come to work with a slight limp and the same dry, grim facial expression that decried her situation with, "Whatever."

At lunch time, she would pull out her purse and say, "Oh, that Bill, he is so in love with me, he just won't stop sending me love letters. Look Bill, I'm not going to write you back until next month, give it a rest." All this with the same dry expression and a slight grin. I worked with Dorothy for about four months before I realized that "Bill" was not a person but a humorous conversation she had with the bills that arrived in her mailbox each day. I loved it and I loved the funny way she handled the continual onslaught of expenses she needed to address each week. I adopted her hilarious expression and amused myself when I received "love letters from bill."

You have countless opportunities to use humor to absorb the shock of your unexpected trials or to quell the fires you will encounter.

Begin with a smile. Have you ever done that before? An uncomfortable smile in response to a situation where you didn't know how to behave? Starting with a smile is better than starting with a loud voice. Start with a smile and then let it rip. Let it explode. What is an exploded smile? Laughter!

> *Good things come to those who wait.*

Chapter 26

THE BEAUTY OF THE WAIT

> Have courage for the great sorrows of life and
> patience for the small ones; and when you have
> laboriously accomplished your daily task, go to
> sleep in peace. God is awake. —VICTOR HUGO

PEOPLE OFTEN CONFUSE PATIENCE WITH TOLERANCE. WHEN
stuck in a line at a discount store, with frustration we tell our
children, "We must be patient." We draw the same conclusion when
stuck in traffic. But patience isn't really determined by how long one
waits, but how you wait. Your attitude during the wait uncovers your
ability to master true patience.

If we could manage every detail of our lives, there would be no
need for patience because we wouldn't force ourselves to wait for anything. But of course we cannot control every facet of our lives; thus
the need for patience.

I'm not certain where you are exactly in the evolution of *your next chapter* or your new dream, but I do know that, irrespective of your place in time, you will need patience to make it to the end. While you wait for the answer from the fourth bank, the judge's decision, or the publisher's response—you need patience for all of those things you cannot control.

Let's begin with an immediate act you can exercise this week. Let's try traffic. No one loves traffic, but you can modify your perspective concerning traffic. Let's use four simple principles which we'll be able to apply to just about anything and obtain the same result.

So you have somewhere important to go; you're cruising along excited about your destination and then you find yourself stuck in traffic. This is synonymous to your new journey. You're cruising along, all is well, and then something you didn't expect shows up and stops you in your steps. What do you do?

The first principle is *proper planning*. I found myself in traffic court many years ago for driving 91 miles per hour on a 55 mile per hour road. I had to stay in court all day because my name began with a "W." By day's end, I had heard many a harrowing story of accidents, vehicular homicides, and out-of-control drivers, mostly young drivers. I listened as the judge lectured on the inability of a driver to control one's car if hit at these accelerated speeds. I was scared straight that day.

I stopped speeding and reconciled that my life was much more important than making it to my destination ten minutes earlier. From that moment on, I began planning better—allowing myself ample time to make it to my destination. If I ran into unexpected traffic, I would still have time to spare.

This simple planning removed significant stress for me when heading out; it will do the same for you. We've already addressed planning in Chapter 6, so you merely need to exercise the same skill during your waiting period.

The second principle is *filling the space*. If you consider again the traffic example and we assume you have planned for this interruption, what do you do while you're waiting? Do you curse, punch the steering wheel, try and weave in and out to gain three feet in front of you, or is there something else you could do?

A temper tantrum is an unproductive, energy-expending waste of time. Instead, I recommend you find a productive and meaningful way to fill the space while you wait. In the car it could be listening to motivational CDs, learning a new language, listening to an audio series that will perfect your use of the English language, like *Verbal Advantage*.

It is a great time for personal development. Or perhaps it's a time to catch up on the telephone with people you never seem to have a chance to speak to. No texting or dialing while driving, of course! Hands-free, stress-free conversation, and before you know it the cars in front of you will begin moving.

You can apply the same exercise to your journey. Fill in the space. Don't drive yourself crazy wondering when someone will call, what they are thinking, or what's going to happen next. Do something! Do something productive, stimulating, alive, and positive. Don't just kill time; it is a commodity you will not be able to get back. Maximize your time; be sure when the car stops you are better because of the wait!

Rationalize your place in time. I remember being held up by my daughter when she was quite young. She had given me the gift of a soiled diaper just as we were supposed to leave the house. It was one of those spills that got all over her dress, her little underpants that covered her diaper, and my rug where she had plopped as I gathered my purse.

I quickly began to clean her up and tried to maintain my frustration as I considered how late I'd be to my television interview well across town. When we got into the car I kissed her big plump cheeks and asked her, "You happy now, poopaface?"

As we traveled outside of my neighborhood onto the main road, I saw flashing lights and caution cones out on the road. There had been a dreadful accident right there where I would normally turn. The officer re-directed us in the opposite direction. I remember praying aloud for the families of the people involved—praying for the health and peace of the people in the car. I didn't know if they had walked away or had perished. I remember in that moment thinking, *That could have been me.* From that moment to this, I tell myself, "I am delayed because I am not supposed to be on the road right now," or, "I'm not supposed to go to the theater tonight."

I do not accept that my life somehow has gone off of the rails because I didn't leave on time or because I missed an important event. Instead, I surmise that I wasn't supposed to be there. If I've done everything right to be at that spot and somehow it didn't come together, God didn't mean for me to be there.

It may be inconvenient or uncomfortable, but begin to accept that, just perhaps, you are exactly where you are supposed to be. It will help increase your patience and give you comfort about the uncontrollable issues of your life.

Remember to move when the traffic moves. Have you ever been at a complete stop and the traffic began to move but you were mentally somewhere else? You only became conscious of your surroundings when the people behind began to beep their horn, alerting you that the congestion ahead had left. We all have had that experience at some time.

After you've done a terrific job at being patient, make sure that when your journey picks up speed and you're nearing the finish line you're not off somewhere else standing behind unmovable obstacles. Stay on guard, be alert, and remember to move when the job of your patience is done. How do you know when it's done? When what you've been waiting for shows up!

> *Mirror, mirror on the wall, who's the fairest of them, y'all?*

Chapter 27

YOUR MIRROR MOMENT

A fair exterior is a silent recommendation.
—PUBLILIUS SYRUS

IF ONLY THE WORLD DIDN'T CELEBRATE BEAUTY, I'D BE A superstar! Anyone can take a great picture; I've done it myself. A great makeup artist, great lighting, and a great photographer can make anyone look good. Believe me, I know from experience. I've had people who've only seen my photo then meet me in person, and you can see the expression on their face change slightly. Don't get me wrong, I'm no beast, but beauty—let's just say I work with what I've got!

The hard truth of the matter is, like it or not, we truly are judged by how we look. You probably know people who have received favorable treatment because of how they look. Beauty matters. Physical appearance matters. It makes no difference what your life calling is.

At some point you will have to encounter people, and therefore how you present yourself will be a critical determining factor in how well you will be received.

I call this section "Your Mirror Moment" because many of us neglect scrutinizing ourselves in the mirror. If we do, oftentimes we feel hopeless concerning our present appearance and conclude there is nothing we can do to change it. I am a great believer in working with what you've got. Everyone has something—a terrific smile, great hair, a great body. A smart presenter knows how to maximize their strengths and minimize their weaknesses.

How well are you displaying your assets? Does anyone even look at you and see an asset? If you are unsure, ask a friend or family member who will be honest with you concerning what they believe is your best physical quality. Ask their opinion as to how you can better present yourself. Look for people like yourself in magazines and see how they play up their physical assets. What's important is to do what you must to continually improve.

I have developed a training called "Looking the Part." On the first day of the training I ask each participant to come dressed as the person they desire to be. For example, I'd have a person opening a catering business and would therefore ask them to look like the type of caterer they desire to be.

I had a participant come as an image consultant, but oddly she didn't look like a person who really mastered her own image. What you desire should match how you present yourself. If you're new on the dating scene, you should leave your home each day as though you want to be noticed. If on the path to be a personal trainer, you should look fit, healthy, and like the kind of person those needing your services want to be. Even authors have to reflect what they are writing about at book signings, interviews, and that infamous back cover photo.

A woman I know who was about 175 pounds overweight said she wanted to write a series of books on weight loss. I really love the concept; having a stage-by-stage evolution of weight loss with the author. The problem was, she had difficulty selling the concept in the title, which had to be relatively brief, and concluding the sale with her picture on the rear.

The publisher liked her but didn't think they could sell the concept. If she were a celebrity, it could have been a home run. But for a first-time author with a great concept, the publisher wasn't willing to take the risk. Why? They argued that people wanting to lose weight wanted to buy success, not simply someone who was still struggling like themselves.

So do a little homework. Find a pictorial model of the person you desire to be. Study their style and see how you can emulate it. Remember, you can't be what you are not; however, you can extract components which you can modify and make your own. Understand that your visual presentation is like a portfolio or business card you leave behind. Your image leaves a lasting impression in the imaginations of those you've met.

I often share a story of a woman in red whom I saw over three decades ago. Her long-enduring image has been seared in my memory. Her example of poise and grace is still a model I emulate when I have to present the total package. I can't remember what the weather was that day, what I was wearing, or how I arrived at McDonald's. In fact, I can't even remember why that eleven-year-old girl strolled into McDonald's that day. I simply recall being third in line.

A man stood at the counter giving his order, making small talk with the cashier. In front of me stood a woman who today I simply refer to as the *woman in red*. She was striking to me. Her petite frame seemed perfect to me in every way, slender and poised in her tailored

red suit. Her jacket landed just below her buttocks and her skirt just above her knee. She wore a sheer white stocking with three-inch high heels. Her blonde hair swooped over the nape of her neck, then danced across her shoulders as if orchestrated to do so. Her wrists were so tiny that the watch on her left hand dangled a bit. Her nails were carefully painted red as though intentionally planned to match her outfit. And oh, my, what a wedding ring.

I imagined what her life must be like. Her husband—did she have children? I guessed she had to be the best kind of mother there was—had to be. Her husband probably greeted her with a kiss each night when he came home.

She had the aroma of wealth. Her fragrance was so distinct, it seemed to tickle my nose. Surely, this was what rich people smelled like. She turned her head gently to the right and I saw her face. She was as beautiful as I imagined. Her skin was like milky white porcelain. How could lips be so red? Or cheeks so gently stained pink?

She was simply exquisite. Impeccable. Divine. In that moment, I knew I wanted to be just like her. Her poise, grace, beauty, and infectious scent. "May I help you?" the cashier asked. The object of my attention seemed to glide to the cashier.

"Coffee, regular."

Just those two words. Nothing else. She looked back at me, as though checking on me, and simply grinned without showing her teeth. She exuded such genuine warmth. *I want that*, I thought.

As an overweight child, I didn't think I could have her slender, petite frame. As a black girl, I thought for sure the blonde hair thing was out and the milky white skin was a definite impossibility. My hands, even at just eleven, seemed more like a lumberjack's than the dainty ring-holders she sported. As a foster child, I knew I was too poor to smell that rich. But as she pivoted and walked away, I knew with certainty that I could glean something to be like this remarkable *woman in red*. "May I help you?" the cashier inquired, breaking my gaze from my oblivious mentor. Just then I realized I had completely forgotten what I was supposed to purchase.

As though by instinct, I clamored, "Coffee, regular." The cashier quickly took my one dollar bill and handed me three silver coins.

"One moment, please," she stammered as she quickly poured the coffee. "Have a good day," she concluded.

"Thank you," I replied, beaming at the thought of having something exactly the same as my *woman in red*. I gently picked it up and attempted to arrange my fingers as she had around the hot cup. I, too, pivoted and walked out. I'm sure I fumbled out, as I had on my way in, but in my mind I was floating across the floor. I wanted so desperately to be her; but if not, I could at least have coffee—regular.

I can only dream of having made such an impression in anyone's life as to be remembered with such detail 30 years later. I am hopeful that you and I can present our best selves to the world and let the imaginations of those we encounter positively run like the wind. I truly hope I can be a *woman in red* to every prospect, every client, and every invisible little girl behind me in line.

> *Your journal is your journey*
> *described in words.*

Chapter 28

JOURNALING YOUR EXPERIENCE

A sentence makes a statement; a paragraph gives a summary; a journal commemorates an experience.

HOW WILL YOU HONOR YOUR JOURNEY? THE TRUTH IS that experience yields hope. As you recall experiences in your life where you've overcome some difficulty, you may be astonished at your strength, at your ability to persevere. Memory is a catalyst to future change. If you can harness your memories to reflect and ponder in the days ahead, they can encourage confidence to do greater things.

Journaling also provides an outlet for the day-to-day or week-to-week tasks, small successes, and ongoing dreams you'll undoubtedly create. Although I write for texts and books fairly easily, I struggle with daily journaling. I journal from experience to experience, writing only those things which I deliberately choose to commit to memory.

I admire people who make the commitment to direct their daily life experiences to paper. I always consider them prolific writers whose biographies have yet been published. You can decide which sort of writer you are, but I recommend you write nonetheless.

Even with my condensed journaling style, I've picked up things I've written in great joy or great pain and have been astounded at who I was during that period. I have often read my writings and questioned if I actually wrote what I was reading; the experience seemed so distant from my present. But most of all, I measured my progression and found that I admired my tenacity at times and treasured the beauty of gentleness I demonstrated during those times of great joy. In short, I marveled at the other woman I read of who proved that I could overcome arduous trials and still maintain the tenderness to be the gentle mother and friend I longed to be.

Experience produces hope. It can make you hopeful that you're capable of doing what you did before and more. It's like the axiom, "If I can get though that, I can get through anything!" Your journal will become a hope chest of possibilities powered by a treasure of experiences—an outpouring of your heart coupled with wisdom you didn't recognize until picked up months or years later.

Here are a few tips to get started:

- Find a beautiful journal. Whether you are a man or a woman, find a journal that is handsome, beautiful, and makes you feel that you are connected with something special.

- If you can, find a special writing instrument. Try to use the same writing instrument all the time. It helps to reinforce the habit and again will make the process of journaling seem distinct.

- Identify a special place to journal—your deck, sitting room, or anywhere you can have privacy.

- Make a decision ahead of time as to how often you will journal. Try not to decide after you've started the process; in fact, put the next date you intend to write as you complete your last entry. It's like making a date with your journal.

Your journal shouldn't have a conclusion; it is not your ending. It should give voice to each new chapter you encounter, word by word, line by line, paragraph by paragraph, chapter by chapter. Kudos to you and the chapter you're writing today and the many chapters you'll see in your tomorrows.